Curries and Spicy Dishes for Your Slow Cooker

Visit Kris Dhillon's website at www.krisdhillon.com and follow her blog at www.thecurrysecret.blogspot.com

Curries and Spicy Dishes for Your Slow Cooker

Kris Dhillon

RIGHT WAY

Constable & Robinson Ltd
3 The Lanchesters
162 Fulham Palace Road
London W6 9ER
www.constablerobinson.com

First published in the UK by Right Way,
an imprint of Constable & Robinson, 2011

A copy of the British Library Cataloguing in Publication Data
is available from the British Library

ISBN: 978-0-7160-2265-7

1 3 5 7 9 10 8 6 4 2

Printed and bound in China

Contents

Photography by Nicholas Christopher

Introduction

WARMING, DELICIOUS and deeply satisfying, slow cooked soups and stews feature in the best cuisines around the world. The epitome of comfort food, I love slow cooked dishes, but until I began writing this book I was not particularly a great fan of the slow cooker. I've owned one for many years and I've found it to be very useful at times but it was not one of my regularly used appliances. I'm not quite sure why, but my perception was that the cooking environment in a slow cooker was not ideal for many of the slow cooked dishes that I've cooked regularly over the years. Well, all that's changed. True, I've had to modify recipes and there has been a bit of trial and error to get the best results, but I now find myself using my slow cooker almost daily. It is so convenient and easy; a few minutes of preparation at the beginning of a busy day and the slow cooker delivers a perfectly cooked meal with little additional time, care or effort.

Though the modern slow cooker has existed for only the last 60 years or so, the concept of slow cooking has been around for centuries. Mankind discovered early that fibrous roots and hard seeds could be softened and tenderized by long, slow cooking and tough, sinewy meat completely transformed; the prolonged low heat breaking down the collagen and allowing the juices to soften the fibres until even the toughest cuts become meltingly tender.

A variety of methods of slow cooking developed in different parts of the world, beginning with people in pre-historic times using slow burning fire pits (these days often referred to as pit ovens), to later generations with their clay pots buried in the dying embers of a fire, or cast iron pots hung over flames and stirred periodically for hours. Indian Americans slow cooked meat wrapped in leaves over a slow open fire and thousands of years later, after colonization, Puritans simmered pots of beans in molasses and cuts of pork all day Saturday to avoid the toil of cooking on the Sabbath. Many of these traditional slow cooking methods are still in use today. Some have evolved into popular modern methods of cooking such as stewing, casseroling, braising and pot-roasting and others are still in use pretty much as they began albeit with the assistance of a little technological advance or two.

Traditional Slow Cooking Techniques

HANGI, A METHOD of slow cooking using heated rocks buried in a pit, originated in the South Pacific region and is still used today on many a special occasion. Hessian, soaked in water, is placed over the hot rocks to create steam. Meat, vegetables and herbs are placed in wire baskets lined with damp cloths and positioned over the hessian. More wet hessian is used to blanket the food and the whole arrangement covered over with layers of soil to completely seal the pit. The combination of moisture in the form of steam, the pressure the steam creates, the direct heat from the rocks and the smoke from dripping fat and burning embers gives hangi food a unique flavour and aroma. Hangi techniques have been handed down the generations and hangi "experts" have emerged who strive to vary and improve the traditional processes.

Dum Pukht is a slow cooking technique dating back to sixteenth century India and possibly beyond, in which food is cooked in sealed, thick bottomed clay pots buried in hot embers for several hours. The large mouth of the spherical pot, sealed with a clay saucer and a hard flour and water paste, is supported by a narrow neck which allows the steam produced in the deep bottom to condense and roll back into the pot maintaining constant moisture throughout the gentle cooking process. The hot steam depicts the *Dum* – warm breath, and *Pukht* means it is "choked" before it can escape, infusing every last morsel of food with deep flavour and aroma. When the seal is broken, the delicious aromas awaken your senses and make your mouth water. This ancient process has now become the most refined form of cooking in many parts of modern India.

The *Tagine*, which is both the name of the unique cooking pot and the dish itself, is widely seen in the cuisines of North Africa. An ingeniously designed cone-shaped lid fits into a flat, circular base with narrow sides. Less tender cuts of meat often combined with several other ingredients such as preserved lemon, dried fruits, honey, olives, spices and a little stock or fruit juice are simmered until the meat is melt-in-your-mouth tender and the flavours deliciously complex. The tall cone of the lid remains cool during cooking, condensing the steam and returning it to the base preventing the food from drying out. When cooking is complete, the lid is removed and the base taken to the table for serving. Traditionally, the tagine is made from heavy clay, often painted in beautiful bright designs before being glazed. These days you're more likely to find tagines with heavy cast iron bases that allow you to brown the meat over high heat before the braising process begins.

The first electric slow cooker was manufactured in Chicago in the 1950s. Somewhat primitive and cumbersome compared to what we have today, it was named the "Naxon Beanery All-Purpose Cooker" or "Beanery" for short, and was primarily developed for cooking baked beans, the national dish of the day. Though contemporary slow cookers are much more sophisticated than their early relative, the principle of the electric slow cooker has changed little in the last 60 years; a metal outer pan, with electric elements at the base and around the sides, houses an inner ceramic pot preventing contact of direct heat with the food and distributing low heat evenly and consistently. There is no need for stirring, watching, checking or supplementing with liquid. The result is that cooks can produce healthy and nutritious food whilst enjoying freedom from the kitchen. The motto – "Cooks all day while the cook's away" – of the 1970s' developer of the slow cooker is even more pertinent in our modern lives.

Benefits of Slow Cooking Your Food

THE BENEFITS OF slow cooking food are as relevant today as they were in the days of our ancestors. Slow cooking is economical, healthy, easy and convenient; a few minutes of preparation in the morning, or the evening before, delivers a nutritious, tasty meal on arriving home from work or after a day out, reducing the temptation to pick up an expensive, fat-laden takeaway. Tougher, cheaper meats can be slow cooked to make them tender and juicy thereby saving you money; and, as the whole meal is cooked in one pot, there is less washing up.

Using a slow cooker to cook your meals also gives you more flexibility with your meal times. If you are running a little late, you don't have to worry about over cooking your food because a little extra cooking time generally will not make any difference. Slow cooking also saves time and effort because you don't need to watch or stir or top up with extra liquid. Just put it on and forget about it.

Slow cooking heats the food gently, keeps it moist and preserves the flavour and goodness giving you a dish with flavours that have time to season and blend with all the ingredients, and meat that is exceptionally tender and juicy.

Slow cookers are relatively inexpensive to buy and because they use little energy, they are also economical to run. No wonder the popularity of the slow cooker continues to grow.

3
What to Expect from Your Slow Cooker

THE MODERN ELECTRIC slow cooker provides a unique way of cooking. Consisting of a round, oval or rectangular outer shell containing thermostatically controlled electric elements and a glazed ceramic or porcelain cooking pot with a well fitting lid, it provides consistent and evenly distributed low heat and a moist cooking environment. Most, if not all, come with at least two heat settings, High and Low, but many also have "Auto" and "Keep Warm" settings which allow the cooker to heat to the High setting at the start of cooking and then automatically turn to Low for the duration of the cooking. The "Keep Warm" setting allows you to keep the food hot until you're ready to eat. Some more advanced models not only switch from cooking to warming automatically, but have programmable timers for switching the cooker off after a pre-set period. Even more sophisticated models have computerized timing devices that allow you to program the entire cooking period at multiple settings of your choice and to delay the start of cooking.

The cooking in a slow cooker happens at a lower temperature compared to other slow cooking methods such as stewing or braising on the hob or in the oven. In the traditional slow cooker the heating element gently heats the food to a steady temperature in the 74°C (low) to 94°C (high) range although, as I've found, newer models heat to higher temperatures to ensure food cooks safely even on the Low setting. The vapour that is produced during cooking continually condenses on the lid and returns to the pot as liquid so it doesn't dry out. In fact, you will often end up with more liquid than you started with because of the juices that are naturally produced when cooking meat and poultry. For this reason the amount of liquid in recipes for the slow cooker is usually significantly less than similar recipes using other cooking methods where some moisture always evaporates.

Because of the low temperatures and high moisture content within the cooking pot, food cooked in a slow cooker remains very moist – much more so than with other slow cooking methods where temperatures are usually a little higher, there is some caramelization and some of the cooking liquid evaporates. This is a tremendous plus when cooking cheaper cuts of meat that have a tendency to dry out when stewed or boiled for a prolonged time at higher temperatures. However, meat cooked in a slow cooker will not brown and, because the fibrous connective tissue softens and stays within the meat instead of dissolving into the cooking liquid, you will not get the richly coloured, flavoursome gravies that are typical of slow cooked curries, stews and braises. To overcome this I always brown meat and onions well and often use a really flavoursome stock in place of water. Some slow cookers conveniently come with a cooking pot that can be placed on the cook top over high heat for browning meat and vegetables before being placed in the slow cooker housing, but a wok or heavy based frying pan can be used instead and the contents transferred to the slow cooker cooking pot.

A slow cooker cooks at temperatures low enough to avoid seriously overcooking food even if you cook it for much longer than recommended but, as with cooking in general, really good results do depend on keeping to the suggested cooking times as closely as possible. Badly overcooked meat and chicken become rather tasteless and vegetables will turn to mush, so if you plan to be out all day, a timer, such as that used for switching lights on and off, can be used to switch the slow cooker off at the desired time ensuring you come home to a beautifully cooked meal.

Getting the Best from Your Slow Cooker

- Always read and follow the manufacturer's instructions and recommendations.
- Get to know your slow cooker – each model is slightly different and, furthermore, newer models cook at higher temperatures compared to older models. This can make a significant difference to the recommended cooking times.

It's best to fill the cooking pot in your slow cooker to a minimum of half full and a maximum of two-thirds full, or according to the manufacturer's instructions. Do not overfill as food can remain uncooked.

If you plan to buy a slow cooker, buy one the right size for your needs so that you don't need either to over fill or under fill.

Use less tender cuts of meat for slow cooking. These are not only cheaper but are much tastier and more suitable for long cooking than more expensive cuts.

Cut each vegetable to about the same size so that they cook evenly.

Root vegetables such as parsnips and carrots take longer to cook at low temperatures than meat so cutting them into pieces smaller than the meat will ensure they are well cooked by the time the meat is done.

Bringing food to boiling point before placing in your slow cooker can reduce cooking time by up to an hour.

Using the "Auto" setting on your slow cooker, or cooking at high for about an hour before reducing to the "Low" setting, better mimics traditional slow cooking methods such as *hangi* and *dum pukht* where the heat in the cooking pit or embers is higher to begin with and gradually decreases over the long cooking period.

If you regularly cook slow cooker meals whilst out for long periods, buying an inexpensive timer to switch your cooker off after the recommended time will ensure that your food is not over cooked.

To stir or not to stir is often a challenge for me if I'm home during cooking – it can be hard to resist. My own experience is that it's not strictly necessary, particularly on the low setting, and will prolong the cooking time but it can help the food cook more evenly when using the High setting. If you want to stir, do it only once about half way through. Repeatedly removing the lid may lower the temperature too much for effective (and safe) cooking. Some manufacturers recommend stirring half way through on the High setting only, so consult your instruction booklet.

How to Get the Best Results when Cooking Curries and Spicy Dishes in your Slow Cooker

WITH A LITTLE MODIFICATION to traditional recipes I have found that it is easy to cook really good curries in the slow cooker. Following the tips below will help to get the best possible results.

- The rich flavour, colour and texture of Indian and many Asian curries depends significantly on the process of frying onions, spices and meats layer by layer in generous amounts of fat before adding any additional liquid. Because the environment in a slow cooker is very moist, it is particularly important to undertake this frying process prior to starting the slow cooking period. Whilst this does mean spending a bit more time in the preparation, the results are well and truly worth it. Most recipes in this book require less than 40 minutes' preparation time and for convenience and flexibility much of it can be done a day or more ahead. Preparing spice mixes, grating or processing items such as garlic, ginger and chillies (and freezing) when you have time to do so will save you time and effort when you cook your curries.

- Curries are typically cooked using liberal amounts of oil or ghee which allows for the essential browning and caramelization of ingredients. It is best to use the full amount of oil recommended in a recipe even if it sounds like there's too much. This will ensure you get delicious rich flavours and colours rather than a boiled taste and an insipid appearance. Skim any excess oil off the top after cooking.

- Spices are key to Indian and Asian curries and the long, moist cooking in the slow cooker dulls the flavour and aroma of ground spices. Adding them in near the end of cooking will give the best results. I recommend about 30–40 minutes before the end of cooking for unroasted ground spices so that they have time to lose that "raw" edge. Spices that have been roasted and ground can be added in just a few minutes before the end. Whole spices, however, can be added at the start as they release their flavours slowly, and either removed before serving or simply moved to the side of the plate when eating.

- Flour is never used for thickening curries. It is the combination of onions, ginger and spices, sometimes with the addition of ground nuts, which provides the thick, rich sauces and gravies typical of these dishes. Sometimes meat based curries are cooked with the same amount in weight of onions to meat resulting in plenty of tasty sauce to eat with rice or bread. It may seem like a lot but it's important not to compromise on the quantity of onions in the recipes.

- When slow cooking meat and poultry dishes, I find that leaving meat on the bone gives better results so most of the recipes in this book recommend using a whole chicken cut into portions (or chicken cutlets) and meat with some bone attached. If you wish to use boned meat reduce the amount by about 20 per cent and use some stock instead of water for extra flavour.

Weights and Measures

BOTH METRIC AND imperial measurements have been given in this book with the imperial measures being rounded up or down to the nearest unit. It's best to use one or the other and not to combine imperial and metric measurements in one recipe.

All spoon measurements throughout the book are **slightly rounded** spoonfuls unless specified as being level.

Fluid ounces refer to the British fluid ounce which is slightly smaller than the US equivalent but the difference is not significant for the recipes in this book.

Cup size is the metric cup (250ml) or about half a British/US pint. Some conversions are given in the tables below:

Measure	UK	USA	Australia
Teaspoon	5 ml	4.93 ml	5 ml
Dessertspoon	10 ml	__	10 ml
Tablespoon	15 ml	14.79 ml	20 ml
Cup	285 ml	236.59 ml	250 ml (metric cup)
Fluid oz	28.41 ml	29.57 ml	__
1 litre	1.75 pints	2.1 pints	

7
Indian/East Asian Dishes

THE FOOD OF THE Indian subcontinent is fabulously unique and diverse. It has evolved over many thousands of years and numerous cultural interactions with neighbouring populations and beyond and in turn has influenced many cuisines around the world, particularly those of Europe and South East Asia.

Indian food is best known for its robust spiciness but not all Indian food is hot; the use of heat imparting chilli varies widely from region to region and personal taste, but all Indian food has the warmth, pungency, aroma and distinct flavour that comes with the use of wonderful spices and fresh and sun-dried herbs.

Slow cooked dishes tend to be the norm in many parts of India. Meat dishes are often made with tough meats such as goat or mutton and simmered for hours with other tasty ingredients and of course the ubiquitous spices. A popular vegetarian dish, Saag, is a mix of fresh mustard greens, spinach and herbs that are simmered for several hours before being pound to a purée and combined with onions, ginger, and green chillies sautéed in hot ghee – known as *Tarka*. Dhal, the common name for a variety of pulses, is a staple throughout India and most varieties need to be cooked long and slow to become sumptuously soft, creamy and digestible.

Ingenious methods of slow cooking developed over the ages. Fuel was often in short supply so slow cooking the next meal in the remnant embers of the cooking fire may well have been borne out of necessity, but it has become a popular cooking method throughout homes and fine restaurants due to the delicious results it produces. I often recall with some nostalgia, having finished a delicious supper cooked on the open fire, watching the cook take a clay pot, fill it with various ingredients, seal the mouth using a clay saucer and flour paste and place it into the hot ashes. Hot embers and ashes were piled onto the top and sides and it was left until breakfast the next day. Just thinking about it now, I can smell the wonderful aromas that wafted across the veranda as the seal was broken and the lid lifted.

Indian Spices and Spice Blends

Spices are the backbone of Indian cuisine. They give Indian food that unique combination of flavours and the warmth, pungency and heat that is distinctive of dishes from this region. A whole range of spices are used in Indian cooking, each with its own unique characteristics.

Whole spices such as cumin, mustard seeds, cinnamon and cardamom are often cooked in hot oil before the meat or vegetables are added. Spice blends (masala), often consisting of nine or more spices, are individually roasted in a hot dry pan before being mixed and ground. Spices roasted in this way are generally added to the dish right at the end as they don't need cooking to take away the raw edge. Blends prepared from unroasted spices are cooked with the main ingredients for a few minutes so that they integrate well into the dish. Curries typically include a number of spices and Indian cooks always have their commonly used spices and spice blends mixed, ground and ready to use in their everyday cooking.

It is best to buy whole spices in quantities that you know you will use within three months or so. Buy spices from an Indian grocer rather than a supermarket because prices are generally lower and the quality a lot better. To ensure maximum taste and aroma, grind only in quantities that are likely to be used up in 3–4 weeks. Store spices in non-reactive containers with tightly fitting lids in a cool, dark and dry place.

Garam Masala

Garam masala is an incredibly aromatic mixture of pungent and warming spices ground to a fine powder. Although recipes for garam masala vary from one region to another and even from household to household, it is widely used in a whole range of Indian curries and foods throughout India. Fussy cooks will grind their garam masala daily but it keeps fine for 3–4 weeks stored in an airtight container.

This is a basic garam masala blend and is ideal for the recipes in this book. The whole spices are not roasted but they do need to be absolutely dry. Putting them out in the hot sun for a few hours or in a low oven for an hour or so helps to ensure that they are.

Makes about 3 tablespoonfuls

1 tbsp coriander seeds
1 tbsp cumin
1 tsp green cardamoms
4 black cardamom pods
1 tsp cloves

1 tsp black peppercorns
2 x 2.5 cm (1 inch) cinnamon sticks
2 bay leaves
½ small nutmeg

• Place all the ingredients into an electric coffee-grinder and grind to a fine powder. Alternatively, grind in a pestle and mortar. Store in an air-tight, non-reactive container.

Indian Curry Powder

Whilst there is no such thing in traditional Indian cuisine, the contemporary Western invention referred to as curry powder is often called for in a variety of curry recipes. You can buy reasonably good powders from supermarkets nowadays but as with any spice blend, you will get better results if you buy good quality whole spices and grind them in small quantities that will be used up within a few weeks.

This blend produces a medium hot powder that can be used in any recipe that requires curry powder.

Makes about 5 tablespoons

1 tbsp coriander seeds
2 tsp cumin seeds
1 tsp fennel seeds
1 tsp fenugreek seeds
1 x 2.5 cm (1 inch) cinnamon stick
1 tsp black peppercorns

6 cloves
½ tsp yellow mustard seeds
8 dried curry leaves (optional)
2 tsp chilli powder
1 tbsp ground turmeric

- Dry roast the whole spices in a small hot pan over low-medium heat, stirring and shaking the pan constantly to ensure they don't burn, for about a minute or until fragrant. Transfer immediately to a plate lined with kitchen paper and cool.
- Combine with the curry leaves (if using) and grind to a fine powder in a pestle and mortar or electric grinder. Add the chilli powder and turmeric and mix well.
- Store in an airtight, non-reactive container.

Chicken and Duck Curries

Traditional Chicken Curry

This delicious, rustic chicken curry was a regular weekend treat when I was growing up. Dad generally cooked the meat curries in our household (with Mum doing all the chopping and washing) and it was quite a ritual; the grinding of spices, the pounding of garlic, ginger and chillies and the slicing of a mountain of onions was a time-consuming business in the days prior to electric food processors and grinders. The resulting curry was spicy and fragrant with lots of really tasty sauce and chicken so tender it was falling off the bone.

Serves 5–6
Preparation time: 30 minutes
Cook time: 2½–3½ hours on High | 5–7 hours on Low

1 chicken (approximately 1.8 kg/4 lb) preferably free range, skinned and chopped into 8 portions plus drumsticks and wings
4 onions, coarsely chopped
8 tbsp ghee or good quality oil
6–7 cloves of garlic, grated or finely chopped
1 large thumb-sized piece of ginger, grated or finely chopped
1½ tsp turmeric
4 ripe tomatoes, chopped or equivalent canned
2 tsp salt or to taste
1 tbsp tomato paste
½ tsp chilli powder or to taste
2 tsp paprika
4 cups (1 litre/1¾ pints) hot water
2–3 green chillies, finely chopped
1½ tsp garam masala
2–3 tbsp chopped fresh coriander

To serve: rice, flat bread such as chapati or nan, vegetable side dish, pickles, raita.

- Rinse the chicken portions well and pat dry with kitchen paper. Place the onion in the bowl of a food processor and process until finely chopped.
- Place the onion in a wok or large pan and add half a cup of water. Bring to the boil and simmer, stirring, until dry, about 5 minutes.

- Add the ghee or oil and stir fry on high heat for about 6–7 minutes until the mixture darkens.
- Add the garlic and ginger, stir fry for a minute or two and add the turmeric. Stir for a few seconds and add the tomatoes and salt. Continue to cook on medium-high heat for about 2 minutes until the tomatoes are soft and pulpy.
- Add the chicken pieces and cook them, turning each piece frequently until all the pieces are sealed. Add the tomato paste and continue to cook, stirring until everything is well mixed and sizzling.
- Stir in the chilli powder and paprika and cook for a further 2–3 minutes. Transfer to the slow cooker. Rinse the pan with 2 cups of the hot water and add to the slow cooker. Stir well.
- Press the chicken pieces into the liquid, adding a little more water if required. Cover and switch on the slow cooker to the desired setting.
- About 30 minutes before the end of cooking, add 1½–2 cups more hot water until you have a good sauce. Stir through the green chillies and the garam masala. Cover and cook on High for the remaining time.
- Allow the curry to stand for a few minutes and spoon off any excess oil. Stir through the coriander and serve.

Shakuti Chicken

Sometimes called Xacuti or Chacuti, the symphony of flavours created by the fragrant spice mix in this delicious Goan dish of tender chicken will get your tastebuds dancing.

Serves 4–5
Preparation time: 30 minutes
Cook time: 3–3½ hours on High | 6–7 hours on Low

Shakuti Spice Paste
1 cup grated coconut, fresh or
    desiccated
6–8 dried Kashmiri chillies (see page 37)
1 tbsp coriander seeds
2 tsp cumin seeds
1 tbsp poppy seeds
1 tbsp sesame seeds
1 x 2.5 cm (1 inch) cinnamon stick
4 cloves
2 tsp fennel seeds
½ tsp black pepper
½ tsp grated nutmeg
1 tbsp oil

4–5 tbsp ghee or good quality oil
1.5 kg (3 lb) chicken, preferably free
    range, skinned and cut into small
    pieces
2 large onions, finely sliced
3–4 cloves of garlic, grated or finely
    sliced
1 thumb-sized piece ginger, grated or
    finely sliced
1 tsp turmeric
½ tsp chilli powder or to taste
2 tsp salt or to taste
1 cup diced fresh tomatoes, or
    equivalent canned
3 cups (750 ml/1¼ pints) hot water
    (approximately)
8 golf ball sized potatoes, peeled or
    2 medium potatoes, peeled and
    quartered
2 tbsp tamarind purée or lime juice
2–3 tbsp finely chopped coriander
    stems and leaves

To serve: basmati rice, flat bread, pickles, raita.

- Heat a little of the ghee or oil in a wok or large pan and lightly brown the chicken pieces, in two batches if necessary to avoid overcrowding, and transfer to the slow cooker.
- Heat the remaining ghee or oil in the same wok or pan and fry the onion until lightly browned, about 6 or 7 minutes.
- Add the garlic and ginger and fry for a minute. Stir in the turmeric, chilli and salt, cook for a few seconds and add the tomatoes. Cook until the tomatoes are pulpy and add to the chicken in the slow cooker.
- Rinse the wok or pan with a little of the water and add to the slow cooker with the remaining water and potatoes. Stir well, pressing the chicken pieces and potatoes into the liquid. Add a little more water if necessary. Cover the slow cooker and switch on to the desired setting.
- Meanwhile, make the paste: dry roast the coconut in a small hot pan over low-medium heat, stirring continuously until golden. This will only take 2 or 3 minutes. Transfer immediately to a plate lined with kitchen paper and cool. Repeat with all the other spice paste ingredients (except for the nutmeg and oil) until the mixture is aromatic (about 2 minutes).
- Grind the cooled spices with the nutmeg to a fine powder using an electric coffee grinder or pestle and mortar. Combine with the oil in the same pan and fry over medium heat for a further 2–3 minutes or until deeply fragrant.
- About 40 minutes before the end of cooking, stir the spice paste and tamarind or lime juice into the chicken and cook on High for the remaining time.
- Stir in the coriander just before serving.

Chicken Bhuna Masala

This tasty curry is spicy but not too hot. It is a popular dish in Indian restaurants where it is generally cooked with boneless pieces of chicken. In this recipe, I've used skinless chicken portions with bone in so that it doesn't cook too quickly and has a richer flavour. The thick flavoursome sauce is delicious with rice or flat bread.

Serves 5–6
Preparation time: 20 minutes or less
Cook time: 2½–3½ hours on High | 5–7 hours on Low

6 tbsp good quality oil
2 large onions, finely sliced
4 cloves of garlic, grated or finely sliced
1 thumb-sized piece of ginger, grated or thinly sliced
1 ripe tomato, chopped
2 tsp salt or to taste
2½ cups (625 ml/20 fl oz) cold water
6 chicken thigh cutlets with bone in, skinned

85 g (3 oz) mushrooms, sliced
1 small green capsicum, sliced
1 tsp turmeric
1 tbsp tomato paste
½ tsp chilli powder or to taste
1 green chilli, finely chopped
1½ tsp garam masala
1 tsp ground cumin
½ tsp dried, ground fenugreek leaves
1 tbsp chopped fresh coriander

To serve: rice, chapati or nan, dhal or vegetable side dish, pickles, yogurt or raita.

- Heat about half the oil in a wok or pan and fry the onion for about 5 minutes or until starting to brown at the edges.
- Add the garlic and ginger and fry for a further minute. Add the tomato and salt and cook for 2–3 minutes until pulpy.
- Add 2 cups of water and, using a stick or jug blender, blend until smooth.
- Transfer to the slow cooker.

- Rinse the chicken pieces and pat dry with paper towels. Heat half the remaining oil in the same pan on high heat and brown the chicken pieces for 3–4 minutes, in two batches if necessary to avoid over-crowding the pan. Place in the slow cooker.

- Heat the remaining oil in the same pan and stir fry the mushrooms and capsicum for 2–3 minutes. Add the turmeric, tomato paste and chilli powder and cook for a further minute. Add to the slow cooker.

- Rinse the pan with the remaining half cup of water and add to the slow cooker. Stir well and switch the slow cooker on to the desired setting.

- About 30 minutes before the end of cooking stir in the green chilli, garam masala, cumin and fenugreek leaves. Cook on High for the remaining time. If the sauce looks too thin, cook uncovered, stirring once or twice.

- Allow the curry to stand for a few minutes and spoon off any excess oil. Stir through the coriander and serve.

Chicken Dhansak

This is a delicious, hearty dish of chicken in a thick lentil sauce flavoured with spices and chilli.

Serves 5–6
Preparation time: 30 minutes or less
Cook time: 3–4 hours on High | 6–8 hours on Low

6 chicken thigh cutlets with bone in (or 8–10 drumsticks), skinned
4 tbsp good quality oil
2 medium onions, finely chopped
3–4 cloves of garlic, finely chopped
1 tbsp grated ginger
1 tsp turmeric
1 ripe tomato, chopped

2 tsp salt or to taste
1 cup red lentils, rinsed and drained
4 cups (1 litre/1¾ pints) hot water
2–3 green chillies, finely chopped
1 tsp garam masala
1 tbsp lemon juice
1 cup pineapple chunks
1–2 tbsp chopped fresh coriander

To serve: rice, flat breads such as chapati or nan, pickles, raita.

- Rinse the chicken pieces and pat dry with paper towels. Heat a tablespoon of oil in a wok or large pan on high heat and brown the chicken pieces for 3–4 minutes, in two batches if necessary to avoid over-crowding the pan. Transfer to the slow cooker.
- Heat the remaining oil in the same pan and fry the onion on medium-high heat for 5–6 minutes, adding a little more oil if required, until starting to brown at the edges.
- Add the garlic and ginger and stir fry for a further minute or two. Stir through the turmeric, tomato and salt. Cook for about 2 minutes more or until the tomato is pulpy. Transfer to the slow cooker together with the rinsed lentils.
- Rinse the pan with a little of the water and add to the slow cooker with all the remaining water. Cover and switch on to desired setting.

- About 30 minutes before the end of cooking, stir in the green chillies, garam masala, lemon juice and pineapple chunks. Add a little more water if the sauce looks too thick and cook on High for the remaining time.
- Stir through the coriander just before serving.

Chicken Madras

Madras, in the south of India has a reputation for robustly spiced, chilli laced dishes. This is a fairly basic curry with the rich flavours and the more than moderate heat that you would expect from the food of this region. Cooking it with chicken pieces including the bone improves the flavour of the tasty thick sauce.

Serves 5–6
Preparation time: 15 minutes or less
Cook time: 2½–3½ hours on High | 5–7 hours on Low

6–8 tbsp good quality oil
2 large onions, sliced
4 cloves of garlic, sliced
1 thumb-sized piece of ginger, sliced
1 ripe tomato, chopped
2 tsp salt or to taste
2½ cups (625 ml/20 fl oz) cold water
6 chicken thigh cutlets with bone in, skinned
1 x 2.5 cm (1 inch) cinnamon stick
6 cardamom pods
1 tsp turmeric
1 tbsp tomato paste
½ tsp chilli powder or to taste
2 green chillies, finely chopped
1 tsp garam masala
½ tsp dried, ground fenugreek leaves
1 tbsp chopped fresh coriander
1 ripe tomato, thinly sliced

To serve: rice, flat bread such as chapati or nan, vegetable side dish, pickles, chutneys, raita.

- Heat about half the oil in a wok or large pan and fry the onion for about 5 minutes or until starting to brown at the edges.
- Add the garlic and ginger and fry for a further minute. Add the tomato and salt and cook for 2–3 minutes until pulpy.
- Add 2 cups of the water and, using a stick or jug blender, blend until smooth. Transfer to the slow cooker.

- Rinse the chicken and pat dry with paper towels. Heat the remaining oil in the same pan and fry the cinnamon and cardamom for about 20 seconds, add the turmeric followed by the chicken.
- Stir fry the chicken on medium to high heat for about 3 minutes until well sealed and stir in the tomato paste and chilli powder. Transfer to the slow cooker.
- Rinse the pan with the remaining half cup of water and add to the slow cooker. Stir well, cover and switch on to the desired setting.
- About 30 minutes before the end of the cooking time stir through the chillies, garam masala and fenugreek. Cook on High for the remaining time. If the sauce looks too thin, cook with the lid off, stirring once or twice.
- Allow the curry to stand for a few minutes and spoon off any excess oil. Stir through the coriander and sliced tomato and serve.

Recipe Notes: The whole spices are not meant to be eaten. Remove before serving or ask your diners to move them to the side of their plates as they eat.

Chicken Jalfrezi

This is a lovely mild curry with a thick sauce and a delicious combination of flavours from the addition of sweet capsicum and ripe, juicy tomatoes.

Serves 5–6
Preparation: 40 minutes or less (plus marinating time)
Cook time: 2½–3½ hours on High | 5–7 hours on Low

6 chicken thigh cutlets with bone in, skinned
1 tsp turmeric
1 tsp grated ginger
½ tsp red chilli powder
6–8 tbsp good quality oil

4 large onions, 2 sliced, 2 cut into 2.5 cm (1 inch) pieces approximately
4 cloves of garlic, sliced
1 thumb-sized piece of ginger, sliced
1 ripe tomato, chopped
2 tsp salt

2½ cups (625 ml/20 fl oz) cold water
1 tbsp tomato paste
1 green capsicum, de-seeded and cut into 2.5 cm (1 inch) pieces
1 red capsicum, de-seeded and cut into 2.5 cm (1 inch) pieces
3–4 medium ripe tomatoes, cut into wedges
1 green chilli or to taste, finely chopped
2 tsp garam masala
Chopped fresh coriander leaves for garnish

To serve: rice, flat bread like chapati or nan, dhal, pickles, chutneys, raita.

- Rinse the chicken pieces and pat dry with paper towels. Place in a non-reactive bowl and sprinkle over the turmeric, grated ginger, chilli powder and a tablespoon of the oil. Mix well, cover and place in the fridge to marinate for 2–3 hours or overnight. Remove the chicken from the fridge about 30 minutes before cooking to allow it to return to room temperature.

- Heat about half the remaining oil in a wok or large pan and fry the sliced onion for about 5 minutes or until starting to brown at the edges.
- Add the garlic and ginger and fry for a further minute. Add the tomato and salt and cook for 2–3 minutes until the tomato is pulpy.
- Add 2 cups of the water and, using a stick or jug blender, blend until smooth. Transfer to the slow cooker.
- Heat a wok or large pan on high heat and brown the chicken pieces for 3–4 minutes or until well sealed and stir in the tomato paste. Cook, stirring for a minute or two and add to the slow cooker.
- Rinse the pan with the remaining water and add to the slow cooker. Stir well, cover and switch on the slow cooker to the desired setting.
- Heat the remaining oil in the same pan over high heat and stir fry the onion and capsicum pieces for 3–4 minutes until opaque. They shouldn't colour. Add the tomatoes and stir fry for a further 30 seconds or so. Set aside.
- About 30 minutes before the end of cooking, stir the vegetables into the chicken together with the green chilli and garam masala. Cook on High for the remaining time.
- Serve sprinkled with the coriander.

Spicy Duck Masala

Duck is perfect for the slow cooker as it needs prolonged gentle cooking to make it really tender. If you're lucky enough to be able to get good duck, this delicious and easy recipe is a really good way to use it.

Duck has a lot of fat under the skin so there will be quite a bit of it floating on top of the sauce at the end of cooking. This can be spooned off before serving or you can reduce the oiliness by removing the skin and discarding it after browning the duck pieces.

Serves 4–5

Preparation time: 40 minutes

Cook time: 4–5 hours on High | 8–9 hours on Low

Spice Blend
1 tsp fennel seeds
1 x 2.5 cm (1 inch) cinnamon stick
4 cloves
6 green cardamoms
1 tsp coriander seeds
1 tsp cumin
½ tsp black peppercorns

1 duck approximately 1.8–2 kg
   (4–4½ lb) in weight
3 onions, roughly chopped

4 large cloves of garlic, peeled and
   chopped
1 thumb-sized piece of ginger, peeled
   and chopped
1–2 tbsp good quality oil
1 tsp turmeric
2 tsp soft brown sugar
2 fresh ripe tomatoes, chopped
1½–2 tsp salt to taste
3 cups (750 ml/1¼ pints) water
2 or more green chillies, finely sliced
½ tsp garam masala
1 tbsp chopped fresh coriander

To serve: rice, flat bread such as chapati or nan, sweet fruit chutney, vegetable side dish, pickles, raita.

- Cut the duck into pieces – 2 thighs, 2 drumsticks and 4 breast pieces. Discard the wing tips. Remove the excess skin and fat, and skin from the sides and ends, leaving only the skin on top of the meat. Rinse well and pat dry with kitchen paper.
- Place the onion, garlic and ginger in the bowl of a food processor and process until finely chopped. Set aside.

- Heat a large heavy based frying pan on medium-high heat and coat with a little oil. Add about half the duck pieces, skin side down, and brown well. Make sure the pan is hot enough and don't overcrowd or the duck will stew rather than brown.
- Turn each piece over and brown on the other side. Transfer the browned duck pieces to the slow cooker and repeat with the remaining duck pieces until all the duck is nicely browned.
- There will be quite a bit of duck fat in the pan by now. Add the onion mixture to it with about a tablespoon of oil and cook on low-medium heat stirring, for about 10 minutes. You don't need to brown the onion but add some more oil if the pan seems too dry.
- Stir in the turmeric followed by the sugar, tomatoes and salt. Turn down the heat a little and cook for 2–3 minutes, stirring once or twice until the tomatoes are pulpy. Add to the duck.
- Rinse the pan with a little of the water and add to the slow cooker with the remaining water. Stir well, cover and switch on the slow cooker to the desired setting.
- Meanwhile, roast the spice blend in a hot dry pan for about a minute or until aromatic. Immediately transfer to a plate lined with a paper towel and cool. Grind the spices to a fine powder.
- About 30 minutes before the end of cooking, stir the ground spices, green chillies and garam masala into curry.
- Stir through the coriander just before serving.

Kerala Duck Curry

The Kerala, known as "the land of spices", is a beautiful Indian state in the south west of the country with sandy beaches, stunning waterfalls, incredible wildlife and a delicious array of hot and intensely spicy foods. Duck is a staple in the backwaters where it is cooked with the ubiquitous coconut, curry leaves and aromatic spice blends and served with rice, often on a banana leaf.

A whole duck, chopped into pieces, is the preferred way for this recipe, but duck portions can be used instead.

Serves 5–6

Preparation time: 30 minutes

Cook time: 4–5 hours on High | 8–9 hours on Low

Spice Blend
2 tsp coriander seeds
1 tsp cumin
6 cardamom pods
6 cloves
1 tsp peppercorns
1 x 2.5 cm (1 inch) cinnamon stick

Grind to a fine powder in a pestle and mortar or electric grinder.

1 duck approximately 1.8–2 kg (4–4½ lb) in weight
4 tbsp coconut oil (or vegetable/olive oil)
3 medium potatoes, peeled and quartered
1 large onion, thinly sliced
4–6 cloves of garlic, finely sliced
1 thumb-sized piece of ginger, grated or finely sliced
6 fresh or dried curry leaves
1 tsp turmeric
2 tsp salt or to taste
400 ml (14 fl oz) can coconut milk
3–4 green chillies, finely sliced
2 tbsp chopped fresh coriander

To serve: rice, flat bread such as chapati or nan, dhal or vegetable side dish, pickles, chutneys, raita.

- Skin the duck and cut into pieces – 2 thighs, 2 drumsticks and 4 breast pieces. Discard the wing tips and remove the excess fat from the sides and ends. Rinse well and pat dry with kitchen paper.
- Heat a large heavy based frying pan on medium-high heat and coat with a little oil. Add about half the duck pieces and brown well. Make sure the pan is hot enough and don't overcrowd or the duck will stew rather than brown.
- Turn each piece over and brown on the other side. Transfer the browned duck pieces to the slow cooker and repeat with the remaining pieces until all the duck is nicely browned. Add the potato.
- Add half the remaining oil to the pan, heat and add the onion. Stir fry over medium-high heat for about 5 minutes until softened, adding a little more oil if needed.
- Add the garlic, ginger and curry leaves and cook, stirring, for a minute or two until aromatic. Stir in the turmeric and salt and add to the duck in the slow cooker.
- Rinse the pan with about half a cup of water and add to the slow cooker.
- Pour off the thick coconut milk from the top of the can and set aside. Add the remaining thin coconut milk to the duck.
- Stir and add a little more water if needed to cover. Switch on the slow cooker to the desired setting.
- About 40 minutes before the end of cooking, stir in the reserved coconut milk, spices and green chillies. Turn up the slow cooker to the High setting for the remaining time.
- Serve garnished with the coriander.

Fiery Goan Duck Vindaloo

Vindaloo is uniquely Goan. The Portuguese term for vinegar (vin) and garlic (ahlo), vindaloo epitomizes the gastronomic Indo-European evolution that has taken place in this region. Whilst the perception is that vindaloo is super hot, the heat should not be the primary force and needs to be in balance with the vinegar and other spicy flavours.

Lamb, goat, pork or beef are delicious in this recipe too.

Serves 4–5
Preparation time: 30 minutes (plus marinating time)
Cook time: 4–5 hours on High | 8–9 hours on Low

Spice paste
10 dried Kashmiri chillies
4–5 dried hot red chillies
2 tsp cumin
1 tsp coriander seeds
1 x 2.5 cm (1 inch) cinnamon stick
1 tsp black peppercorns
4 cloves
2 tsp turmeric
6 cloves of garlic, roughly chopped
1 thumb-sized piece of ginger,
    roughly chopped
4 tbsp dark balsamic (or other)
    vinegar

1 duck approximately 1.8–2 kg
    (4–4½ lb) in weight
4 tbsp good quality oil or ghee
3 medium onions, finely chopped
2 cups (500 ml/18 fl oz) hot water
    (approximately)
2 tsp salt or to taste
2–3 green chillies, finely chopped
½ tsp garam masala

To serve: rice, flat breads such as chapati or nan, dhal or vegetable side dish, pickles, chutneys, raita.

- Grind the dried chillies and whole spices to a fine powder in a coffee grinder or pestle and mortar and combine with the turmeric. Place the garlic, ginger and vinegar in a blender jug and blend until smooth. Add to the ground spices and mix well.

- Skin the duck and cut into pieces – 2 thighs, 2 drumsticks and 4 breast pieces. Discard the wing tips and remove the excess fat that hangs from the sides and ends. Rinse well and pat dry with kitchen paper. Place in a non-reactive bowl large enough to hold the duck comfortably.
- Add the spice paste to the duck and mix until all the pieces are well coated with the paste. Cover and refrigerate for at least 8 hours or overnight. Remove from the fridge about 30 minutes before cooking to allow the duck to return to room temperature.
- Heat the oil or ghee in a wok or large pan and fry the onion for about 5 minutes on medium to high heat until softened.
- Turn up the heat to maximum and add the duck and marinade. Stir fry for 5–6 minutes until the moisture evaporates and it starts to release the oil. You may need to turn down the heat a little towards the end to stop the mixture catching to the bottom. Transfer to the slow cooker.
- Rinse the pan with the hot water and add to the duck together with the salt. Stir well and switch the slow cooker on to the desired setting. Add a little more hot water if required to cover.
- Stir through the green chillies and garam masala about 30 minutes before the end of cooking and cook on High for the remaining time.

Recipe Notes:
- Kashmiri chillies have a deep red colour and mild flavour. They are available in dried form, whole and ground, from Indian grocers.
- This recipe produces a medium-hot curry. Increase the amount of dried hot chilli or add chilli powder for a hotter flavour.

Chicken Korma

This mildly spiced curry is rich, creamy and delicious. The ground almonds not only thicken the sauce but also add a lovely flavour.

Serves 5–6
Preparation time: 15 minutes
Cook time: 2½–3½ hours on High | 5–7 hours on Low

4 tbsp good quality oil
2 large onions, sliced
4 cloves of garlic, sliced
1 thumb-sized piece of ginger, sliced
1 ripe tomato, chopped
2 tsp salt
2½ cups (625 ml/20 fl oz) cold water
6 chicken thigh cutlets bone in, skinned

1 tsp turmeric
2 tsp tomato paste
½ tsp chilli powder
1 tsp ground cumin
½ tsp garam masala
½ tsp ground cardamom
2 tbsp ground almonds
4 tbsp double cream
1 tbsp chopped fresh coriander

To serve: rice, flat bread like chapati or nan, a vegetable side dish, pickles, chutneys, raita.

- Heat about half the oil in a wok or large pan and fry the onion for about 5 minutes or until just starting to brown at the edges.
- Add the garlic and ginger and fry for a further minute. Add the tomato and salt and cook for 2–3 minutes until pulpy.
- Add the water and, using a stick or jug blender, blend until smooth. Transfer to the slow cooker.
- Rinse the chicken portions and pat dry with paper towels. Heat the remaining oil in the same pan on high heat and brown the chicken pieces for 3–4 minutes or until well sealed.
- Stir in the turmeric, tomato paste and chilli. Cook, stirring, for a minute or two and transfer to the slow cooker.
- Rinse the pan with a little water and add to the slow cooker. Stir well and switch the cooker on to the desired setting.
- About 30 minutes before the end of cooking stir through the cumin, garam masala, cardamom, ground almonds and cream. Cook on High for the remaining time.
- Serve sprinkled with the coriander.

Lamb/Mutton/Goat Curries

Traditional Rogan Josh

In the native (Persian) language, Rogan means "clarified butter" and Josh means "hot", so essentially Rogan Josh is meat – lamb, goat or beef – cooked with clarified butter at high heat. The origins of this immensely popular dish lie around the early sixteenth century with the magnificent Moghuls who introduced opulence in living and dining, hitherto unknown to India.

The relentless heat of the Indian plains frequently drove the Moghul emperors to the cooler mountain air of Kashmir where the Indian version of Rogan Josh is thought to have been created. The fiery red appearance of the dish traditionally comes from the liberal use of the mildly flavoured but deeply red Kashmiri chilli, although some modern recipes use paprika or even red food colouring for the same effect.

Recipes vary widely, but an authentic Rogan Josh should be aromatic and not too hot.

Serves 5–6
Preparation time: 40 minutes
Cook time: 4–5 hours on High | 8–9 hours on Low

1 kg (2¼ lb) boneless leg of lamb, cut into 4 cm (1½ inches) chunks
4 tbsp plain yogurt
1 tsp turmeric
8 tbsp ghee or good quality oil
8 cardamom pods
6 cloves
1 x 2.5 cm (1 inch) cinnamon stick
3 bay leaves, fresh or dried
4 medium onions, finely sliced
4–5 cloves of garlic, finely chopped
1 thumb-sized piece of ginger, finely chopped

2 tsp salt or to taste
1 tbsp tomato paste
2 tsp Kashmiri chilli powder (or 1 tsp chilli powder and 1 tsp paprika)
1 tsp of hot chilli powder or to taste
1½ cups (375 ml/12 fl oz) hot water (approximately)
1 green chilli, finely chopped
½ tsp garam masala
1 ripe tomato, sliced
2 tbsp chopped fresh coriander

To serve: rice, flat bread such as chapati or nan, dhal or vegetable side dish, pickles, raita.

- Combine the lamb, yogurt and turmeric in a non-reactive bowl and set aside.
- Meanwhile heat the ghee or oil in a large, heavy based saucepan and add the whole spices and bay leaves. Stir once and add the onion. Stir fry the onion for about 8 minutes over high heat or until golden.
- Add the garlic and ginger and cook for 1 or 2 minutes until aromatic. Add the lamb mixture and stir fry on high heat until all the liquid evaporates and the oil is released, about 3–4 minutes.
- Turn down the heat a little. Stir in the salt, tomato paste and chilli powders and stir until incorporated. The mixture should be a deep red now. Transfer to the slow cooker.
- Rinse the pan with the hot water and add to the lamb. Stir well, cover and switch the slow cooker on to the desired setting.
- About 30 minutes before the end of the cooking time, stir in the green chilli, garam masala and sliced tomato.
- Allow the curry to stand for a few minutes and spoon off any excess oil before serving.
- Serve garnished with coriander.

Recipe Notes: The whole spices are not meant to be eaten. Remove before serving or ask diners to move them to the side of their plates.

Bhuna Gosht
(Dry Lamb Curry)

Bhuna, roughly translated means "roasted" or "dry fried"; therefore a Bhuna Gosht is a curry of lamb, or more usually mutton, stir fried with spices resulting in a sauce so thick it just clings to the tender meat morsels like an intensely flavoursome dark and spicy gravy.

The rich flavour of this dish comes from cooking the meat in its own juices with the spices and little additional liquid, and then frying until quite dry and roasted. This means a little more effort but the result is a delicious curry that is wonderful with rice or chapati.

Serves 5–6
Preparation time: 30 minutes or less (plus marinating time)
Cook time: 3–4 hours on High | 6–8 hours on Low

2 small onions, roughly chopped
1 thumb-sized piece of ginger, roughly chopped
6 cloves of garlic, roughly chopped
½ cup (125 ml/4 fl oz) fresh plain yogurt
1 kg (2¼ lb) lamb or mutton with some bone, cut into about 5 cm (2 inch) pieces
½ tsp turmeric
5–6 tbsp good quality oil
2 bay leaves

2 black cardamoms
1 x 2.5 cm (1 inch) cinnamon stick
6 cloves
2 cups (500 ml/18 fl oz) hot water (approximately)
2 tsp salt or to taste
2 tsp ground coriander
1 tsp chilli powder or to taste
3 green chillies, finely sliced
1 tbsp tomato paste
1 tsp garam masala
1 tbsp chopped fresh coriander

To serve: rice, chapati, dhal or vegetable side dish, pickles and raita.

• Place the onion, ginger, garlic and yogurt into the bowl of a food processor or blender and process until fairly smooth.

42

- Place the lamb in a non-reactive bowl and add the yogurt mixture and turmeric and stir well until all the meat pieces are well coated. Cover and refrigerate for 2 hours or overnight. Remove from the fridge about 30 minutes before required to allow the meat to return to room temperature.
- Heat half the oil in a wok or pan and fry the bay leaves and whole spices for about 5 seconds. The oil should be hot enough to sizzle as soon as the spices are dropped in.
- Add the meat mixture to the oil and spices and stir fry until the meat browns lightly, about 3 minutes. Transfer to the slow cooker.
- Rinse the wok or pan with about half a cup of hot water, add to the meat, stir in the salt, cover and switch the slow cooker on to the desired setting and cook until the meat is tender but not falling apart.

  (You can prepare the dish to this stage up to a day ahead).

- Heat the remaining oil in a wok or large pan and ladle the contents of the slow cooker into it. Stir fry over high heat for 3–4 minutes until most of the liquid evaporates.
- Turn down the heat a little and add the ground coriander, chilli powder and green chillies. Stir fry for a further 3–4 minutes, adding a splash or two of water to prevent the mixture catching if necessary. The meat and sauce should be nicely browned and releasing the oil by this stage.
- Add about half a cup of hot water, the tomato paste and garam masala and stir fry until most of the liquid evaporates again.
- Add the remaining water, bring to the boil and simmer gently for a further 2–3 minutes.
- Serve sprinkled with the coriander.

Recipe Notes: The whole spices are not meant to be eaten. Remove before serving or ask diners to move them to the side of their plates when eating.

Traditional Lamb Dhansak

A traditional dhansak is a deliciously healthy dish of meat, two or three different types of lentils and several vegetables cleverly cooked into a taste sensation of hot, sour and slightly sweet flavours.

As with all recipes, ingredients and cooking methods vary from region to region and even from one household to another, but the basic requirements are the same throughout – lamb, goat or mutton, a range of lentils, pumpkin, aubergine, chillies and spices.

Serves 5–6
Preparation time: 40 minutes
Cook time: 3–4 hours on High | 6–8 hours on Low

5–6 tbsp good quality oil
1 kg (2¼ lb) lamb loin chops, trimmed and each cut into 2 pieces
2 onions, finely chopped
1 thumb-sized piece of ginger, grated
4–5 cloves of garlic, finely chopped
1 tsp turmeric
2½ tsp salt or to taste
2 ripe tomatoes, chopped
1 tsp chilli powder
1 cup lentils (red, toor, green or a combination)
1 cup grated pumpkin or sweet potato
1 small aubergine, finely diced
5 cups (1.25 litres/2¼ pints) hot water
1½ tsp garam masala
½ tsp dried kasoori methi (optional)
2–3 green chillies, finely chopped
1 tbsp jaggery, palm sugar or soft brown sugar
2 tbsp tamarind purée or lime juice
2 tbsp chopped fresh coriander

To serve: rice, chapatis, pickles, raita.

- Heat a little oil in a wok or pan and brown the meat in two or three batches. Transfer to the slow cooker.
- Heat the remaining oil and fry the onion for 5–6 minutes until starting to brown. Add the ginger and garlic and stir fry for about two minutes until aromatic.

- Stir in the turmeric and salt and add the tomatoes and chilli powder. Cook over medium heat until the tomatoes are pulpy. Transfer to the slow cooker. Rinse the pan with one cup of the water and pour over the meat and onion.
- Add the lentils and vegetables to the slow cooker with the remaining water. Stir well, cover and switch on the slow cooker to the desired setting.
- About 30 minutes before the end of cooking, add all the remaining ingredients except for the coriander and stir through.
- Cook on High for the remaining time. Serve sprinkled with the coriander.

Recipe Notes:

- The pumpkin or sweet potato and aubergine should melt into the well cooked lentils. Grating, processing or cutting them up really small helps to do that.
- Jaggery is boiled down sugar cane juice – the raw sugar before it's refined. Palm or soft brown sugar is a good alternative.

Gosht Dopiaza
(Lamb with Onions)

Do means "two" and Piaza is the Indian word for "onions", so Gosht Dopiaza is lamb or mutton cooked with two lots of onions.

Considering how good it is, this is quite an easy recipe.

Serves 5–6

Preparation time: 40 minutes or less

Cook time: 3–4 hours on High | 6–8 hours on Low

1 thumb-sized piece of ginger, roughly chopped
6 cloves of garlic, roughly chopped
½ cup (125 ml/4 fl oz) fresh plain yogurt
6–8 tbsp good quality oil
1 kg (2¼ lb) lamb or mutton with some bone, cut into about 5 cm (2 inch) pieces
1 x 2.5 cm (1 inch) cinnamon stick
6 cardamom pods

6 whole cloves
5 large onions, 2 finely chopped, 3 sliced into thin half rings
½ tsp turmeric
2 tsp salt or to taste
1 tsp chilli powder to taste
1½ cups (375 ml/12 fl oz) hot water
2 tsp ground coriander
2 tsp ground cumin
½ tsp garam masala

- Place the ginger, garlic and yogurt into the bowl of a food processor or blender, add about half a cup of cold water, and process until fairly smooth. Set aside.
- Heat a little of the oil in a wok or large pan and brown the meat lightly, in two batches if necessary to prevent overcrowding. Transfer to the slow cooker.
- Heat half the remaining oil in the same wok or pan and add the whole spices. Stir for 5 seconds and add the finely chopped onion.

- Stir fry on high heat for about 5 minutes. Stir in the turmeric and add the yogurt mixture. Cook, stirring on high heat until all the water evaporates. Continue to fry for about a minute more over low heat.
- Stir through the salt, chilli powder, and hot water. Cover and switch the slow cooker onto the desired setting.
- About 40 minutes before the end of the cooking time, heat the remaining oil and fry the sliced onion over medium heat for about 10 minutes or until golden. Stir in the coriander and cumin and cook for a further minute.
- Add to the slow cooker with the garam masala and stir in. Cook on High for the remaining time.
- Allow the curry to stand for a few minutes and spoon off any excess oil before serving.

Recipe Notes: The whole spices are not meant to be eaten. Remove before serving or ask diners to move them to the side of their plates.

Shahi Korma
(Lamb in Cream and Almond Sauce)

This dish of tender lamb in a cardamom and saffron flavoured creamy sauce, thickened with ground almonds, epitomizes the opulence of Moghul cuisine. It's an impressive dish that is fairly mildly spiced and really delicious, perfect for a special occasion.

Serves 5–6
Preparation time: 45 minutes or less
Cook time: 3–4 hours on High | 6–8 hours on Low

4 tbsp good quality oil

2 large onions, finely sliced

4 cloves of garlic, minced or finely chopped

1 thumb-sized piece of ginger, grated or finely chopped

1 ripe tomato, chopped

2 tsp salt or to taste

2½ cups (625 ml/20 fl oz) cold water

1 x 2.5 cm (1 inch) cinnamon stick

8 cardamom pods, lightly crushed

1 kg (2¼ lb) boneless leg of lamb, cubed

1 tsp turmeric

1 tsp chilli powder

2 tsp coriander seeds

1 tsp cumin

½ tsp black peppercorns

½ tsp garam masala

1 cup (250 ml/8 fl oz) double cream

2 tbsp almonds, ground to a powder

1 tsp saffron

2 tbsp hot milk

1 tbsp toasted flaked almonds to garnish (optional)

To serve: rice, flat bread such as nan or chapati, a dhal or vegetable side dish, pickles, chutneys, raita.

- Heat just over half the oil in a wok or large pan and fry the onion for about 5 minutes over high heat until starting to brown at the edges.
- Add the garlic and ginger and fry for a further minute. Add the tomato and salt and cook for 2 or 3 minutes until pulpy.

- Add 2 cups of the water and blend the mixture until smooth using a stick or jug blender. Transfer to the slow cooker.
- Heat the remaining oil in the same pan and add the cinnamon and cardamom pods. Fry for 5 or 6 seconds and add the meat. Stir fry for 3–4 minutes until browned.
- Stir in the turmeric and chilli powder, cook for a few seconds and transfer to the slow cooker.
- Rinse the pan with the remaining water and add to the slow cooker. Cover and switch on to the desired setting.
- Meanwhile, dry roast the coriander, cumin and peppercorns in a small hot pan, stirring and shaking the pan constantly to ensure they don't burn, for about a minute or until fragrant. Transfer immediately to a plate lined with kitchen paper and cool. Grind to a fine powder.
- About 30 minutes before the end of cooking add the spice mixture to the slow cooker with the garam masala, cream and ground almonds. Stir well and cook on High for the remainder of the time. Soak the saffron in the hot milk.
- Stir the saffron and milk through the curry. Allow to stand for about 5 minutes and serve sprinkled with the flaked almonds if using.

Lamb Pasanda

Pasand or *Pasanda* means "liked" or "to like" and Lamb Pasanda is a dish that tends to be liked by all, young and old, due to its delicious creamy consistency and mild spice flavours. It is a very aromatic and tasty dish, even if you prefer your food hot. Just have some extra chopped chilli on the table for chilli lovers.

Serves 5–6

Preparation time: 45 minutes (plus marinating time)

Cook time: 3–4 hours on High | 6–8 hours on Low

Marinade Ingredients

3 onions, roughly chopped

1 thumb-sized piece of ginger, roughly chopped

6 cloves of garlic, roughly chopped

½ cup (125 ml/4 fl oz) fresh plain yogurt

½ tsp chilli powder

1 tsp turmeric

1 tsp paprika

1 tsp dried kasoori methi leaves

1 kg (2¼ lb) boneless leg of lamb

5–6 tbsp ghee or good quality oil

2 tsp salt or to taste

2 cups (500 ml/18 fl oz) hot water

2 tsp ground coriander

1 tsp ground cumin

4 tbsp single cream

4 tbsp almonds, finely ground

1 green chilli, finely sliced

1 tsp garam masala

2 tbsp chopped fresh coriander

To serve: rice, chapati or nan, vegetable side dish, pickles, raita.

- Place all the marinade ingredients in the bowl of a food processor or blender and process until fine.
- Trim and slice the lamb thinly. Place each piece between two sheets of plastic wrap and beat with a meat mallet or rolling pin until flattened. Cut into 5 cm x 2.5 cm (2 inch x 1 inch) strips.

- Combine the marinade and lamb in a non-reactive bowl, mix well, cover and refrigerate for at least 2 hours or overnight. Remove from the fridge about 30 minutes before required.

- Transfer the lamb mixture to the slow cooker and stir in about half the ghee or oil and the salt. Rinse the bowl out with about a cup and half of the hot water and add to the lamb. Stir, cover and switch the slow cooker on to the desired setting and cook until the meat is tender but not falling apart.

(The dish can be cooked to this stage up to a day ahead.)

- Heat the remaining ghee or oil in a wide, heavy based pan and add the cooked meat and juices. Cook over high heat until nearly all the liquid evaporates.

- Turn the heat down to medium and continue stir frying until the mixture darkens and releases the oil, about 5 minutes

- Add the ground coriander and cumin and stir fry for a minute or so until the spices are aromatic.

- Add the remaining half cup of hot water and all the remaining ingredients except for the fresh coriander. Simmer gently for 2 minutes.

- Allow the curry to stand for a few minutes and spoon off any excess oil. Stir through the coriander and serve.

Keema Mattar
(Spicy Minced Lamb with Peas)

This simple dish of deliciously spiced minced lamb and peas is one of my favourites. It is wonderful served with freshly cooked chapatis and a cooling home-made yogurt or raita. The traditional way to make it is with lamb but it is equally good with minced pork.

Serves 4–5

Preparation time: 40 minutes or less

Cook time: 3–4 hours on High | 6–8 hours on Low

4–5 tbsp good quality oil
1 kg (2¼ lb) lean minced lamb
3 onions, finely chopped
3–4 cloves of garlic, minced or finely chopped
1 large thumb-sized piece of ginger, grated or finely chopped
1 tsp turmeric
1 tsp ground cumin

400 g (14 oz) can chopped tomatoes
2 tsp salt or to taste
1 tbsp tomato paste
1 tsp chilli powder or to taste
2 tsp paprika
1 tsp garam masala
2–3 green chillies, finely chopped
1½ cups frozen baby peas
2–3 tbsp chopped fresh coriander

To serve: chapati, raita or yogurt, raw onion, pickles, dhal or vegetable side dish.

- Heat a tablespoon of oil in a wok or large pan and lightly brown the meat, stirring and breaking up the lumps. Transfer to the slow cooker.
- Heat the remaining oil and fry the onion over high heat for 5–6 minutes or until lightly golden. Add the garlic and ginger and stir fry for a minute or two.
- Stir in the turmeric and cumin and cook for a few seconds before adding the tomatoes and salt. Cook the tomatoes for 3–4 minutes until some of the liquid evaporates and the tomatoes are thick and pulpy.

- Add the tomato paste, chilli powder and paprika. Stir fry for a minute or so and stir into the meat in the slow cooker. Cover and switch the slow cooker on to the desired setting. Stir half way through cooking if possible.
- About 30 minutes before the end of cooking, add the garam masala, green chillies and frozen peas. Cook on High for the remaining time.
- Stir through the coriander and serve.

South Indian Mutton Curry

South Indian cuisine is renowned for its generous but balanced use of spices. Curries are typically very hot, often incorporating three or four different types of chilli, but other complex spicy flavours are evident from the inclusion of ingredients such as cardamom, nutmeg, peppercorns and cloves. I have toned down the heat in this recipe but the amount of chilli could easily be doubled for authentic tastes.

Mutton is the preferred meat for flavour and economy, but it may be difficult to get, so goat or even lamb can be used instead.

Serves 5–6
Preparation time: 30 minutes (plus marinating time)
Cook time: 3–4 hours on High | 6–8 hours on Low

1 kg (2¼ lb) mutton (with some bone) cut into chunks
1 tsp chilli powder or to taste
1 tsp turmeric
2 tbsp lemon juice
3 tbsp ghee or good quality oil
1 large onion, finely sliced
2 tsp salt or to taste
1 tbsp tomato paste
2 cups (500 ml/18 fl oz) hot water
1 tsp garam masala
1 tbsp chopped fresh coriander

Wet Spice Paste
1 x 2.5 cm (1 inch) cinnamon stick
2 cloves
6 cardamom pods
½ tsp poppy seeds (khus khus)
1 tsp cumin seeds
1 tsp coriander seeds
½ tsp black peppercorns
small piece nutmeg

2–3 green chillies
2 tsp grated coconut (fresh or dried)
6 cloves of garlic, coarsely chopped
1 thumb-sized piece of ginger, coarsely chopped

1 tbsp oil

To serve: rice, flat bread such as chapati or nan, dhal or vegetable side dish, pickles, chutneys, raita.

- Combine the mutton, chilli powder, turmeric and lemon juice in a non-reactive bowl and place in the fridge to marinate for about an hour or overnight. Remove from the fridge about 30 minutes before cooking to allow it to return to room temperature.
- Heat the ghee or oil in a wok or large pan and fry the onion for about 5 minutes until starting to brown.
- Add the meat and cook for 3–4 minutes, stirring, until the meat pieces are well sealed and add the salt, tomato paste and water.
- Transfer to the slow cooker, cover and switch to the desired setting.
- Meanwhile, dry roast the first eight ingredients of the Wet Spice Paste in a small hot pan, stirring and shaking the pan constantly to ensure they don't burn, for about a minute or until fragrant. Transfer immediately to a plate lined with kitchen paper and cool.
- Grind the spices to a fine powder in a mortar and pestle or electric coffee grinder.
- Process the green chillies, coconut, garlic and ginger in a small food processor or pound in a pestle and mortar, adding a splash of water, until you have a fairly smooth paste. Add the ground spices and process or pound until well combined. Refrigerate until required.
- About 40 minutes before the end of cooking, heat the tablespoon of oil in a small pan and fry the spice paste for a minute or two until aromatic.
- Stir into the curry together with the garam masala. Cover and cook on high for the remainder of the cooking time.
- Allow the curry to stand for a few minutes and spoon off any excess oil. Stir through the coriander and serve.

Indian Goat Curry

Goat is a popular meat for curries throughout India. It can be tough but it is very flavoursome and cooked slowly becomes really tender, so it is perfect for the slow cooker.

This robust curry is a delicious mix of spicy flavours that are enhanced by the tang of the fresh yogurt. Like most slow cooked meat dishes, you get the best flavour by leaving some bone in during cooking. I've made this curry with both forequarter (shoulder) chops and leg meat. In the latter case I've removed the meat from the bone and diced it and then cooked the bone with the meat for added flavour. I prefer shoulder meat as it is more succulent but either will do.

Serves 4–5

Preparation time: 30 minutes

Cook time: 6–8 hours on High | 3–4 hours on Low

Whole Spice Mix

1 tsp cumin

1 tsp fennel seeds

6 green cardamom pods

1 black cardamom

1 bay leaf

1 x 2.5 cm (1 inch) cinnamon stick

8 cloves

5–6 tbsp good quality oil

3 large onions, thinly sliced

1 thumb-sized piece of ginger, grated or finely chopped

4–5 cloves of garlic, grated, minced or finely sliced

2 tsp salt or to taste

1 tsp chilli powder

1 tsp turmeric

1 kg (2¼ lb) goat meat (including some bone) cut into 3 cm (just over 1 inch) chunks

1 cup (250 ml/8 fl oz) fresh plain yogurt, stirred until smooth

1 cup (250 ml/8 fl oz) hot water (approximately)

2–3 green chillies, finely sliced

½ tsp garam masala

To serve: rice, flat bread such as chapati or nan, dhal or vegetable side dish, pickles, chutneys, raita.

- Heat the oil in a pan large enough to hold the meat in a single layer and fry the whole spice mix for about 5 seconds. The oil should be hot enough so that the spices start to sizzle and pop on contact with the oil.
- Immediately add the onion and cook over high heat for 3–4 minutes until softened.
- Stir in the ginger and garlic and stir fry for a minute or so until aromatic. Add the salt, chilli powder and turmeric and stir in.
- Keeping the heat high, add the goat pieces and cook, stirring, for 4–5 minutes until the meat is really well sealed.
- Drizzle over about a third of the yogurt and stir fry until the liquid evaporates. Repeat with half the remaining yogurt and again with the remaining yogurt, cooking until each addition is absorbed.
- Add the hot water, stir well and transfer to the slow cooker, cover and switch on to the desired setting.
- About 40 minutes before the end of cooking, stir in the green chillies and garam masala. Cook on High for the remaining time.
- Allow the curry to stand for a few minutes and spoon off any excess oil before serving.

Indo-Fijian Goat Curry

Fijian cuisine is a delicious fusion of the robust spicy flavours of India with local foods like coconut, fish, sweet potatoes and cassava. Cooking styles are simpler compared to Indian cooking methods, with everything being more or less "thrown together" rather than the frying of ingredients layer by layer typical of Indian cooking – perfect for easy slow cooker meals.

Serves 5–6
Preparation time: 30 minutes
Cook time: 3–4 hours on High | 6–7 hours on Low

6–8 cloves of garlic, coarsely chopped
1 red or green chilli, coarsely chopped
3 onions: 2 coarsely chopped, 1 finely chopped
2 strips lime zest
3 cups (750 ml/1¼ pints) water (approximately)
2 tbsp ghee or olive oil
2 tsp chilli powder or to taste
1 tsp turmeric
2 tsp sugar

1 lime, juiced
2 tsp salt or to taste
1 kg (2¼ lb) goat meat (with some bone) cut into chunks
2 medium potatoes, peeled and quartered
2 carrots, peeled and diced
2 tbsp curry powder (page 18)
1 cup chopped coriander leaves and stems
½ cup (125 ml/4 fl oz) yogurt, stirred until smooth

To serve: rice, coconut chutney, a fish or vegetable dish, raita.

- Place the garlic, chilli, coarsely chopped onion, lime zest and water into a blender jug and blend until smooth.
- Transfer to a medium saucepan. Rinse the jug with a little more water, add to the pan and bring to the boil. Add the ghee or oil, chilli powder, turmeric, sugar, lime juice and salt and let the sauce simmer for a minute or two.
- Meanwhile place the meat and vegetables in the slow cooker. Pour over the hot sauce and stir well, pressing the meat and vegetables into the liquid. Cover the slow cooker and switch on to the desired setting.
- About 40 minutes before the end of cooking stir through the curry powder and half the coriander. Cook on High for the remaining time.
- Stir through the finely chopped onion and yogurt and serve sprinkled with the remaining coriander.

Beef and Pork Curries

Pakistani Beef and Potato Curry

Rich and flavoursome, Pakistani cuisine is often described as a blend of the various cuisines of the region. This is a wholesome but easy recipe with tender chunks of beef in a rich, thick sauce. Don't be tempted to skimp on the onions and use a good quality, preferably homemade garam masala for the best tasting curry.

Beef is the popular meat for Pakistani style curries but lamb or goat can be used instead.

Serves 5–6

Preparation time: 30 minutes

Cook time: 3–4 hours on High | 6–8 hours on Low

3 large onions, sliced

6 cloves of garlic, sliced

1 thumb-sized piece of ginger, sliced

8 tbsp good quality oil

1 tsp turmeric

1 kg (2¼ lb) lean boneless stewing beef, cut into large chunks

3 medium potatoes, peeled and each cut into 4 pieces

2 tbsp tomato paste

2 tsp salt or to taste

2 tsp chilli powder or to taste

3 cups (750 ml/1¼ pints) hot beef stock or water

1½ tsp garam masala

1–2 tbsp chopped coriander

To serve: rice, wheat bread, dhal or vegetable side dish, pickles, chutneys, raita.

- Place the onion, garlic and ginger in the bowl of a food processor and process until fine.
- Transfer to a wok or pan and add about a cup of water. Bring to the boil and simmer over low heat for about 5 minutes until the onion is soft and the water has evaporated.
- Add the oil and fry the onion mixture for 5–6 minutes until beginning to brown. Add the turmeric, stir and add the beef. Cook,

stirring, for 2–3 minutes and add the potatoes. Stir fry for a further 2 minutes or so.

- Stir in the tomato paste, salt and chilli powder and stir fry for a minute. Stir through a cup of stock or water and transfer to the slow cooker. Rinse the pan with the remaining stock or water and add to the meat.
- Stir well, cover and switch the slow cooker on to the desired setting.
- About half an hour before the end of cooking, stir in the garam masala.
- Allow the curry to stand for a few minutes and spoon off any excess oil. Stir through the coriander and serve

Pork Tikka Masala

Pork is quite a popular meat in the Punjab and this dish is a variation of the dry, spicy and oily Pork Tikka which is served at the ubiquitous Punjabi dhabas or roadside restaurants. Chunks of pork shoulder are marinated and slowly cooked until very tender and the whole lot stir fried with an aromatic onion mixture and generous amounts of spices until the juicy meat chunks are coated in a thick spicy sauce.

Serves 5–6

Preparation time: 15 minutes (plus marinating time)
Cook time: 3–4 hours on High | 6–8 hours on Low

Marinade
3 onions, coarsely chopped
6–8 cloves of garlic, coarsely
   chopped
1 thumb-sized piece of ginger,
   chopped
1 cup (250 ml/8 fl oz) plain yogurt
1 tsp chilli powder
1 tsp salt
1 tbsp good quality oil

1.2 kg (2½ lb) pork leg or shoulder,
   cut into chunks
½ cup (125 ml/4 fl oz) hot water
6 tbsp good quality oil
1 tsp turmeric
2 green chillies, finely chopped
1 tsp ground cumin
1 tsp ground coriander
1 tsp paprika
1 tsp salt or to taste
1½ tbsp garam masala
2 tbsp chopped fresh coriander

To serve: chapatis or other flat bread, dhal, pickles, chutneys, raita or plain yogurt.

- Process or finely chop the onion, garlic and ginger. Reserve about half of the onion mixture and combine the rest with the remaining marinade ingredients. Add the pork to the marinade and refrigerate for at least 2 hours or overnight if time allows.

- Transfer the meat and marinade to the slow cooker, add the water and mix well. Cover and switch the slow cooker on to the desired setting and cook until the meat is very tender but still holding its shape.

  (The dish can be prepared to this stage up to 24 hours ahead.)

- Heat the oil in a wok or large pan and add the reserved onion mixture. Stir fry for 4–5 minutes on medium-high heat until starting to brown.

- Add the cooked meat and juices. Cook on high for 4–5 minutes until about half the liquid has evaporated.

- Turn down the heat to medium, add all the remaining ingredients except the garam masala and chopped coriander, and stir fry the meat and spices for a further 3–4 minutes until dark. You should have a richly coloured thick sauce by now and it will be releasing the oil.

- Stir through the garam masala and cook, stirring, for a further minute or two until the sauce is very thick.

- Let the curry stand for a few minutes, during which time it will thicken further. Spoon off excess oil if preferred and serve sprinkled with the coriander.

Winter Pork and Vegetable Curry

This curry is delicious and satisfying. I like to make it with pork shoulder, bone in, cut into large chunks and combined with tasty winter vegetables like turnips and sprouts but it is also good with spinach or a combination of spinach, potatoes and carrots. Use fresh, seasonal vegetables and cook until really tender and the meat is falling off the bone.

Serves 6–7
Preparation time: 30 minutes
Cook time: 4–5 hours on High | 8–10 hours on Low

350 g (12 oz) Brussels sprouts
1 large or two small turnips
½ cup (125 ml/4 fl oz) good quality oil
4 medium onions, thinly sliced
2 large knobs ginger, grated
4–5 cloves of garlic, minced or finely chopped
1 kg (2¼ lb) pork shoulder, cut into large chunks

1½ tsp turmeric
1 x 400 g (14 oz) can chopped tomatoes or equivalent fresh
2½ tsp salt or to taste
1 tsp chilli powder
1 cup (250 ml/8 fl oz) water
2–3 green chillies
2 tsp garam masala

To serve: chapatis or nan, dhal, pickles, raita.

- Trim and slice the sprouts into equal sized pieces, halving the small ones and cutting the larger ones into 3 or 4 pieces. Peel and slice the turnip into 2 cm (just under 1 inch) chunks. Place in the slow cooker.
- Heat the oil in a wok or large pan and fry the onion for about 5 minutes, until starting to brown. Add the ginger and garlic and cook for a minute or so until aromatic.

- Add the meat, sprinkle over the turmeric and stir fry on high heat for 4–5 minutes until the meat is well browned.
- Stir in the tomatoes and salt and continue to cook, stirring over medium-high heat for 2–3 minutes until much of the liquid has evaporated and the oil is released.
- Stir in the chilli powder and transfer to the slow cooker. Rinse the wok or pan with the water and add to the meat and vegetables. Stir well, cover and switch the slow cooker on to the desired setting.
- About 30 minutes before the end of cooking, stir in the green chillies and garam masala. Let the curry stand for a few minutes and serve.

Goan Beef Vindaloo

Goan cuisine is a rich and delicious blend of Portuguese and local flavours. This easy-to-cook curry typifies the robust flavours of this region. The heat of a vindaloo should be balanced with the vinegar and other spices.

Serves 5–6
Preparation time: 25 minutes
Cook time: 3–4 hours on High | 6–8 hours on Low

Spice Paste
2 tsp cumin
2 tsp coriander seeds
6–8 hot dried red chillies, according to taste
1 tsp black peppercorns
6 cardamom pods
2 tsp fenugreek seeds
1 tsp mustard seeds
½ tsp sugar
1 tsp turmeric
3 tbsp balsamic or brown vinegar

3 medium onions, coarsely chopped
6 cloves of garlic, coarsely chopped
1 thumb-sized piece of ginger, coarsely chopped
1 kg (2¼ lb) stewing beef, cut into large chunks
6 tbsp good quality oil
2 tsp salt or to taste
2 cups (500 ml/18 fl oz) hot water

To serve: rice, nan, dhal or vegetable side dish, pickles, chutneys, raita.

- Grind all the whole spices and sugar to a fine powder and combine with the turmeric and vinegar.
- Process the onion, garlic and ginger until finely chopped and combine with the meat, oil and spice paste in a large bowl. Mix well.
- Heat a wok or large saucepan on high heat and brown the meat mixture well in two or three batches. Transfer to the slow cooker. Add the salt and about half the water.
- Rinse the pan with the remaining water and add to the slow cooker. Stir well. Cover and switch the slow cooker on to the desired setting and cook until the meat is really tender.
- Let the curry stand for a few minutes and spoon off any excess oil.

Spicy Fish and Vegetable Curry

This is a healthy and nutritious east Indian recipe that is mildly hot but very aromatic and flavoursome. Fish does not take long to cook but cooking the vegetable "stew" slowly with the spices makes it a really tasty base for the quick cooking fish. You can vary the vegetables according to what is in season and at its best.

Serves 6–7
Preparation time: 30 minutes
Cook time: 3–4 hours on High | 6–8 hours on Low

Spice Blend
½ tsp fenugreek seeds
1 tsp black mustard seeds
1 tsp onion seeds
1 tsp fennel seeds
1 tsp cumin seeds

1½ tsp turmeric
1 tsp chilli powder
750 g (28 oz) firm fleshed white fish
    sliced into large pieces
2 large onions, coarsely chopped
6 cloves of garlic, coarsely chopped
1 thumb-sized piece of ginger,
    coarsely chopped

6 tbsp good quality oil
2 tsp salt or to taste
4 tbsp fresh, plain yogurt
3 medium potatoes, peeled and
    quartered
1 small aubergine, cut into chunks
    slightly larger than the potato
2 cups (500 ml/18 fl oz) hot water
1 cup frozen peas
½ tsp garam masala
2–3 green chillies, deseeded and
    sliced lengthways (optional)

To serve: rice, chapatis or nan, pickles, chutneys, raita.

• Sprinkle a little of the turmeric and chilli powder over the fish pieces, mix well, cover and refrigerate until required.

- Process the onion, garlic and ginger until finely chopped. Heat all but 1 tablespoon of the oil in a wok or large pan and add the spice blend. When the seeds begin to pop, add the onion mixture and fry on high heat for 5–6 minutes until lightly browned.

- Stir in the remaining turmeric, chilli powder and salt followed by half the yogurt. Continue to cook over high heat until all the moisture evaporates, about a minute. Repeat with the remaining yogurt.

- Add all the vegetables except for the frozen peas and stir to coat in the spice mixture. Lower the heat a little and cook, stirring, for about 2 minutes. Transfer to the slow cooker.

- Rinse the pan with the hot water and add to the slow cooker. Stir well, cover and switch the slow cooker on to the desired setting.

- About 30 minutes before the end of cooking, stir in the frozen peas. Heat the remaining oil in a wok or pan and fry the fish pieces for a minute or two until very lightly browned. Add to the slow cooker with the garam masala and stir gently to combine. Cover and cook on High for the remainder of the time until the fish is cooked through.

- Serve sprinkled with the green chillies if using.

Fish Curry with Coconut and Coriander

Fresh seafood and sweet coconuts are abundant in the southern Indian state of Kerala and this popular fish dish combines both ingredients beautifully. It is simple to prepare and full of flavour due to the tangy tamarind and robust spices.

Use any firm fleshed white fish such as ling, cod, swordfish or king fish or try it with salmon, prawns or a combination of seafood.

Serves 5–6

Preparation time: 20 minutes

Cook time: 2–2½ hours on High | 4–5 hours on Low

1 kg (2¼ lb) fish fillets
1½ tsp salt or to taste
1 tsp turmeric
2 tsp chilli powder or to taste
4 tbsp good quality oil
2 tsp yellow mustard seeds
1 tsp fenugreek seeds
1 medium onion, finely sliced
8 curry leaves fresh or frozen
3 cloves of garlic, finely sliced

1 tbsp grated ginger
1 tbsp ground coriander
2 tsp ground cumin
3 tbsp tamarind purée dissolved in ½ cup warm water
1 cup grated fresh coconut (or unsweetened desiccated)
1 cup (250 ml/8 fl oz) coconut milk
1½ cups (375 ml/12 fl oz) water
2–3 tbsp chopped fresh coriander

To serve: rice, chapati or nan, vegetable or dhal side dish, pickles, chutney, raita.

- Rinse the fish fillets and pat dry with paper towels. Slice each fillet into 4 or 5 equal sized pieces. Place on a large plate.
- Combine the salt, turmeric and chilli powder and sprinkle over the fish. Mix to coat and set aside for about 10 minutes.
- Heat the oil in a wok or large pan and add the mustard and fenugreek seeds. When they start popping add the onion and curry leaves. Fry over high heat until lightly browned, about 5 minutes.
- Add the garlic and ginger and stir fry for a minute or two until aromatic. Stir in the coriander and cumin and fry for a few seconds. Add the tamarind, coconut, coconut milk and water, stir and transfer to the slow cooker.
- Add the fish pieces, stir, cover and switch the slow cooker on to the desired setting. Stir half way through cooking.
- Serve sprinkled with the coriander.

Goan Prawn Curry

Goan food is a delicious blend of Portuguese cuisine with the local foods and flavours of the Indian south/west coast. This is an incredibly easy recipe that can be prepared in 10 minutes but is impressive enough for a special occasion.

Serves 5–6
Preparation time: 10 minutes
Cook time: 2–2½ hours on High | 4–5 hours on Low

2 tbsp coriander seeds
1 tbsp cumin
3 tbsp good quality oil
1 small red capsicum, diced
6 cloves of garlic, finely chopped
1 tbsp grated ginger
1 tsp turmeric
1½ tbsp paprika

1 tsp chilli powder or to taste
2 green chillies, finely chopped
1½ tsp salt or to taste
2 tbsp tomato paste
2 cups (500 ml/18 fl oz) coconut milk
800 g (28 oz) large fresh prawns,
    peeled
2 tbsp lime juice

To serve: rice, nan, pickles, chutneys, raita.

- Grind the coriander and cumin to a fine powder.
- Heat the oil in a wok or pan and fry the capsicum for a minute over high heat. Add the coriander and cumin and fry for 30 seconds.
- Stir in the garlic and ginger and stir fry for a minute or two until aromatic. Add all the remaining ingredients except for the lime juice, stir well and transfer to the slow cooker.
- Cover the slow cooker and switch on to the desired setting and cook until the prawns are cooked through. Stir through the lime juice just before serving.

Fish Kalia

The delicious slow cooked, aromatically spiced sauce in this popular Indian seafood dish is flavoured with a special spice blend called Panch Phoran (five spices). Any firm fleshed fish can be used including salmon or trout.

Serves 6
Preparation time: 30 minutes
Cook time: 4–5 hours on High | 8–10 hours on Low

Spice Blend
¾ tsp fenugreek seeds
1½ tsp black mustard seeds
1½ tsp onion seeds
2 tsp fennel seeds
2 tsp cumin seeds

2 tsp turmeric
6 fish cutlets or fillets about 200 g
   (7 oz) each
2 large onions, coarsely chopped
6 cloves of garlic, coarsely chopped
1 thumb-sized piece of ginger,
   coarsely chopped

6 tbsp good quality oil
2 tsp salt or to taste
1 cup (250 ml/8 fl oz) fresh, plain
   yogurt
2 tbsp tomato paste
2 tsp paprika
3 cups (750 ml/1¼ pints) hot water
3 ripe tomatoes sliced into thin wedges
   (or 6 cherry tomatoes halved)
3–4 hot red chillies, de-seeded and
   sliced
1 tsp garam masala
3–4 tbsp chopped fresh coriander

To serve: rice, chapati or nan, pickles, chutneys, raita.

- Sprinkle about half the turmeric over the fish and rub in, cover and refrigerate until required.
- Process the onion, garlic and ginger until finely chopped.
- Heat the oil in a wok or large pan and add the spice blend. Stir around in the hot oil for about 10 seconds until the seeds start to

pop and add the onion mixture. Stir fry for about 5 minutes until starting to brown.

- Stir in the remaining turmeric and salt followed by about a third of the yogurt. Stir fry until all the liquid evaporates. Repeat with the remaining yogurt a couple of tablespoons at a time until all of it is incorporated.
- Add the tomato paste, cook for a minute and add the paprika. Stir in about half the water and transfer to the slow cooker. Rinse the wok or pan with the remaining water and add to the slow cooker. Cover and switch on to the desired setting.
- About an hour before the end of cooking, heat a large frying pan capable of holding at least half the fish in a single layer. Cook each piece on high heat for a minute each side or until lightly browned.
- Transfer the fish to the slow cooker, sprinkle over half of the red chilli and half of the garam masala and turn the pieces in the sauce until each piece is completely coated. Cover and cook on High for the remaining time until the fish is cooked through.
- Stir in the tomato slices. Transfer to a serving platter or plates, sprinkle with the remaining red chillies, garam masala and coriander. Serve.

Vegetables and Dhals

Fijian Courgette and Chana Dhal

In Fiji this hearty vegetarian dish is made with a type of gourd called lauki. In the Indian version a type of squash (sometimes called Chinese Melon) about the size of a small marrow with a pale green skin is used. Yellow or pale green courgettes (zucchini) or button squash are good substitutes. It is a tasty dish that is quite spicy to provide a lively lift to the relatively mild tasting basic ingredients.

You can reduce the cooking time by half by soaking the dhal in cold water over night.

Serves 6–7 as a main dish, more as a side dish
Preparation time: 15 minutes
Cook time: 6–7 hours on High | 12–14 hours on Low

1½ cups split chana dhal (split chickpeas) or yellow split peas
5 cups (1.25 litres/2¼ pints) hot water
1 tsp turmeric
2 yellow or pale green courgettes (zucchini) or 4 button squash
2 tsp salt or to taste
3 tbsp ghee or extra virgin olive oil
2 medium onions, finely sliced

2 tsp cumin seeds
2 tsp mustard seeds
4 cloves of garlic, finely sliced
1 tsp chilli flakes
2–3 green chillies, finely sliced
1 thumb-sized piece of ginger, finely sliced
1 lime or lemon, juiced
2 tbsp chopped fresh coriander

To serve: chapati or nan, yogurt, pickles, salad.

- Wash the dhal in two or three changes of water and drain. Add to the slow cooker with the water and turmeric. Cover and switch the slow cooker on to the desired setting.
- About 30 minutes before the end of cooking, halve the courgettes lengthways and cut each length into 1 cm (just under ½ inch) thick slices. Or slice each button squash into 6 slices. Add to the slow cooker and stir in the salt. Cook on High for the remainder of the time.
- Meanwhile, heat the ghee or oil in a frying pan and add all the remaining ingredients except for the lime or lemon juice and coriander. Stir fry on medium heat for about 5 minutes.
- Stir the onion mixture into the dhal with the lime or lemon juice and coriander and serve.

Mixed Vegetable Curry

This is a tasty and healthy curry of vegetables in a thick spicy sauce. It is good as a vegetarian dish with yogurt or raita, or perfect as a side dish with a meat curry. Use the freshest, tastiest vegetables you can find for the best results.

Serves 6 as a main dish or more as a side dish
Preparation time: 30 minutes
Cook time: 3–4 hours on High | 6–8 hours on Low

3 medium onions, coarsely chopped
4–6 cloves of garlic, coarsely chopped
1 thumb-sized piece of ginger
6 tbsp good quality oil or ghee
1 tsp turmeric
4 ripe tomatoes, chopped
2 tbsp grated fresh coconut (or unsweetened desiccated)
2 tsp salt or to taste
1 tsp paprika
2 medium potatoes, peeled and quartered

2 carrots, diced
1 aubergine (about 200 g/7 oz) sliced into chunks a bit larger than the potato
1 cup button mushrooms, halved
2 cups (500 ml/18 fl oz) hot water (approximately)
1 cup frozen peas
3 green chillies or to taste, finely sliced
1 tsp garam masala
½ tsp dried methi (optional)
2 tbsp chopped fresh coriander

To serve: chapati or nan, meat, chicken or fish curry, pickles, chutneys, raita.

- Process the onion, garlic and ginger until finely chopped.
- Heat the oil or ghee in a wok or large pan, and fry the onion mixture on high heat for about 8 minutes until golden. Add the turmeric, stir in and add the tomatoes. Cook for 2–3 minutes until pulpy.

- Add the coconut, stir fry for a few seconds and add the salt and paprika. Stir and add all the vegetables except the frozen peas. Sauté the vegetables for 2–3 minutes on medium heat and add a cup of water.
- Mix well and transfer to the slow cooker. Rinse the pan with the remaining hot water, add to the vegetables and stir. Cover and switch the slow cooker on to the desired setting.
- About 30 minutes before the end of cooking, stir in the peas, chillies, garam masala and methi if using. Cook on High for the remainder of the cooking time.
- Serve the curry sprinkled with the coriander.

Aloo Mattar
(Potato and Pea Curry)

This is a simple but delicious north Indian recipe of potatoes and peas in a thick, spicy sauce. It is often eaten as a main dish with yogurt or raita but is also good as a side dish with meat, chicken or fish.

Serves 5–6 as a main dish or more as a side dish
Preparation time: 35 minutes
Cook time: 3–4 hours on High | 6–8 hours on Low

6–8 tbsp good quality oil
2 large onions, coarsely chopped
4–6 cloves of garlic, sliced
1 thumb-sized piece of ginger, sliced
6 ripe tomatoes (or equivalent canned), chopped
2 tsp salt, or to taste
4 cups (1 litre/1¾ pints) cold water
1 x 2.5 cm (1 inch) cinnamon stick
6 cardamom pods
2 bay leaves

6 medium potatoes, peeled and quartered
1 tsp turmeric
2 tsp paprika
2 cups frozen peas
3–4 green chillies, finely chopped
1½ tsp garam masala
1 tsp dried fenugreek leaves (optional)
2 tbsp chopped fresh coriander

To serve: chapati or nan, meat, chicken or fish curry, pickles, chutneys, raita.

- Heat about half the oil in a wok or pan and fry the onion for about 5 minutes or until starting to brown at the edges.
- Add the garlic and ginger and fry for a further minute. Turn down the heat a little and add the tomato and salt and cook for a minute or two until pulpy.
- Stir in the water and, using a stick or jug blender, blend until fairly smooth. Transfer to the slow cooker.

- Heat the remaining oil in the same wok or pan and add the cinnamon, cardamom pods and bay leaves. Stir fry for about 10 seconds and add the potatoes.
- Cook the potatoes over medium heat for about 3 minutes, turning regularly until very lightly browned. Sprinkle over the turmeric and cook for 20–30 seconds more. Add to the slow cooker.
- Rinse the pan with a little water and add to the slow cooker. Sprinkle over the paprika, stir and switch the slow cooker on to the desired setting.
- About 40 minutes before the end of cooking, add the peas, chillies, garam masala, and fenugreek (if using). Stir and cook on High for the remaining time.
- Stir through the coriander just before serving.

Recipe Notes: Remove whole spices before serving or ask your diners to move them to the sides of their plates.

Chana Masala

Chickpeas are nutritious and versatile and a good, cheap source of protein. They are widely consumed throughout India and Asia in an array of different preparations ranging from nibbles and snacks to main dishes with potatoes and other ingredients.

Chana Masala is a delicious dish with hot and tangy flavours often served at festive occasions with fried breads (puri or bhatura) and spicy meat or potato filled samosas.

Serves 4–5 as a main dish or more as a side dish
Preparation time: 30 minutes or less
Cook time: 3–4 hours on High | 6–8 hours on Low

4–5 tbsp good quality oil or ghee
2 large onions, grated or finely chopped
3–4 cloves of garlic, minced or finely chopped
1 large thumb-sized piece of ginger, grated or finely chopped
1 tsp turmeric
2 tsp salt or to taste
2 cups chopped ripe tomato (or canned)

1½ cups chickpeas, soaked overnight and drained
1 tsp paprika
3 cups (750 ml/1¼ pints) hot water
2–3 green chillies, finely sliced
1 tsp dried fenugreek leaves
1 tsp garam masala
1 tbsp Chana Masala spice mix*
2 tbsp chopped fresh coriander

To serve: puri, bhatura or samosas, yogurt or raita, sliced raw onion seasoned with salt and freshly ground pepper, fresh mint and lime or lemon juice.

- Heat the oil or ghee in a wok or large pan and fry the onion for about 5 minutes or until lightly golden.
- Add the garlic and ginger and stir fry for a minute or two. Stir through the turmeric and salt and add the tomatoes. Cook, stirring, for 3–4 minutes until the tomatoes are pulpy.

- Add the chickpeas and stir fry for a further 3–4 minutes or until most of the liquid has evaporated.
- Stir through the paprika and transfer to the slow cooker. Rinse the wok or pan with the water, add to the slow cooker, cover and switch on to the desired setting.
- About 30 minutes before the end of cooking, stir through the chillies, dried fenugreek, garam masala and Chana Masala mix. Cook on High for the remaining time.
- Allow to stand for about 10 minutes, stir through the coriander and serve.

★ Chana Masala spice mix is available from most Indian grocers. If you cannot get it, use 1 tsp each of chilli powder, ground cumin and coriander. Also add either 2 tsp ambchoor (green mango powder) or 1 tablespoon tamarind purée.

Punjabi Marrow Curry

If you have never eaten marrow curry before, believe me you're in for a treat. It is a delicious combination of robust flavours and textures against the juicy softness of the mild flavoured marrow. The fenugreek seeds and leaves are responsible for those zappy "curryish" flavours and are vital for this recipe. The additional spicy flavours come from generous quantities of garlic, ginger and chilli and the texture from a Punjabi ingredient called Bhadi (sometimes spelt Wadi), a sundried "cake" of ground, fermented and spiced moong dhal that is a key component of this dish. All ingredients are readily available from Indian grocers.

Serves 4–6 as a vegetarian main dish, more as a side dish
Preparation time: 30 minutes
Cook time: 3–3½ hours on High | 6–7 hours on Low

6 tbsp good quality oil
½ tsp fenugreek seeds
60 g (2 oz) butter or ghee
4 onions: 2 finely chopped, 2 thickly sliced
4–6 cloves of garlic, minced or finely chopped
1 thumb-sized piece of ginger, grated or finely chopped
Small knob of ginger, julienned
2 ripe tomatoes, chopped
2 tsp salt (or to taste)

1½ tsp turmeric
1 marrow (approximately 1 kg/2¼ lb in weight) peeled, and chopped into chunks, including pith and seeds
2 Punjabi bhadi, each one broken into 3 or 4 pieces
3–4 green chillies, finely chopped
1 tbsp dried fenugreek leaves (khasoori methi)
1 tsp garam masala
2 tbsp chopped fresh coriander (optional)

To serve: flat breads like chapati, mountain bread or parathas, yogurt or raita, pickles.

- Heat the oil in a large, heavy based saucepan and add the fenugreek seeds. If the oil is hot enough they should start to pop within a few seconds. Be careful not to burn them as they will turn bitter.

- Immediately stir in the butter or ghee and add the onion. Cook the onion for about 10 minutes, stirring regularly, until it softens and starts to brown at the edges.
- Add the garlic and all the ginger. Cook for about a minute and stir in the tomato, salt and turmeric. Cook, stirring, for another minute or two, and add the marrow and Punjabi bhadi.
- Stir well and transfer to the slow cooker. Rinse the pan with about half a cup of water and add to the slow cooker. Stir again, cover and switch on the slow cooker to the desired setting.
- About 30 minutes before the end of cooking, stir in the chillies, fenugreek leaves and garam masala. Cook on High for the remainder of the cooking time, with the lid off if there is too much liquid.
- Serve sprinkled with the fresh coriander if using.

Dhal Makhani

This is a very satisfying and nourishing dhal popular throughout India. It requires long, slow cooking to soften the hard pulses so it is ideal for the slow cooker. Once cooked it is flavoured with the Tarka – onions, garlic and spices cooked in hot oil or ghee and mixed into the dhal. Because it takes so long to cook, Indian households generally make enough for two or three days. Each subsequent day before serving, a smaller tarka is prepared and combined into the dhal and each day the dhal becomes even tastier.

Traditionally, this dish is made using generous quantities of butter and ghee. I generally use a healthy combination of extra virgin olive oil with a relatively small amount of butter for my dhal but you can use one or the other and vary the quantities as you wish. But maybe just once indulge yourself and savour it with a generous knob of good quality butter.

Serves 4–5 as a vegetarian main dish or more as a side dish
Preparation time: 15 minutes
Cook time: 6–7 hours on High | 12–14 hours on Low

½ cup urad dhal
½ cup moth dhal*
6 cups (1.5 litres/2½ pints) hot water
2 tsp salt or to taste
1 tsp dried ground ginger

Tarka
4 tbsp extra virgin olive oil
90 g (3 oz) good quality butter

1 small onion, finely chopped
2–3 cloves of garlic, minced or finely
    chopped
1 thumb-sized piece of ginger, grated
2–3 green chillies, finely chopped
1 tsp garam masala
1 tsp turmeric
1 tbsp chopped fresh coriander
    (optional)

To serve: rice or flat breads such as chapati or paratha, pickles, raita.

- Pick the dhal over for stones, wash in a couple of changes of water and place in the slow cooker. Add the water and switch on to the desired setting.
- When the dhal is cooked add the salt and dried ginger and give it a really good stir to make a nice creamy texture.
- Heat the oil and butter for the tarka on medium heat and fry the onion for 6 or 7 minutes until softened and starting to brown at the edges.
- Add the garlic, ginger and chilli and stir fry for 2 minutes or until fragrant. Stir in the garam masala and turmeric and fry for a minute more.
- Add the tarka to the dhal and stir until it is well incorporated. Stir in the fresh coriander if using, and serve.

Recipe Notes: The dhal naturally thickens on cooling. Just add a little water when reheating until you have the desired consistency.

*Moth dhal is a light brown pulse similar in shape to urad (which is black) but slightly smaller. It is readily available from Indian grocers but you can use urad dhal alone if preferred.

Tarka Dhal

Serves 3–4 as main dish, more as a side dish
Preparation time: 10 minutes
Cook time: 3–4 hours on High | 6–8 hours on Low

1 cup good quality red split lentils
4½ cups (1.125 litres/2 pints) cold
    water
1 onion, finely chopped
3 cloves of garlic, finely chopped
2 tsp grated ginger
3 tbsp extra virgin olive oil or ghee

½ tsp turmeric
1 ripe tomato, chopped
2–3 green chillies, finely chopped
1½ tsp salt or to taste
½ tsp garam masala
1–2 tbsp finely chopped fresh
    coriander

- Rinse the lentils in two or three changes of water and place in the slow cooker with all the other ingredients except the chilli, salt, garam masala and coriander.
- Cover and switch the slow cooker on to the desired setting.
- About 30 minutes before the end of cooking, stir in the chilli, salt and garam masala.
- Stir through half the coriander and sprinkle with the remaining coriander just before serving.

Thai/South East Asian Dishes

THE FOOD OF THAILAND and South East Asia is a true culinary paradise of tastes and aromas. There is less use of dried spices than in Indian food and more of fresh, deeply fragrant herbs. It is vibrant, colourful and artistic in presentation and delivers flavours that are both intensely flavourful and subtly complex. Sweet, sour, salty, bitter and hot flavours blend harmoniously to delight the diner at every meal.

As with Indian and east Asian food, the cuisine of this region is a product not only of its soils and climate but of its history and geography, the religious beliefs and cultural sensibilities of its people and of the degree of wealth or poverty. Major influences are present from India to the West – introducing aromatic, spicy curries – and from China and the East offering noodles and wok cooking. The most profound contributors, the Portuguese, are believed to have introduced chilli to the region in the sixteenth century and its fiery heat is omnipresent at every meal. Whilst each country in the region has retained its own distinct culinary identity there are many common staple ingredients such as rice, noodles, coconut milk, chilli, lemongrass, coriander and comparable cooking methods such as stir frying and of course slow cooking to utilize cheaper, tougher cuts of meat.

Curry Pastes

Curry pastes are to the food of this region what spice blends are to the curries of the Indian sub-continent, perhaps even more so. A good curry paste made with the best ingredients is, therefore, very important for really great curries. Fortunately, modern kitchen appliances like food processors and blenders make them easy to prepare so if you have the time to make your own pastes, it is well worth it. Otherwise, a commercial preparation can be supplemented with fresh ingredients like coriander, garlic, lemongrass and lime leaves so that you can maximize the delicious, intense flavours and aromas typical of these curries.

Curry pastes keep well in the fridge for up to a week and can be frozen for up to six months, so prepare enough for three or four curry recipes when you have the time.

Recipe Notes:
• If you are going to keep the paste in the fridge for any length of time, pour just enough oil over the top of it to cover. This will help keep the paste fresh.
• Be careful when handling chillies, wear thin rubber gloves or wash your hands thoroughly and do not touch your eyes.

Red Curry Paste

This rich red paste can be used in a range of curries and soups. It is typically very hot, too hot for most western tastes, but you can reduce the heat by using a milder variety of chilli like the Kashmiri chilli which will give you the rich red colour without the heat.

If you are making this paste using a pestle and mortar, using coarse sea salt helps to grind down all the ingredients.

Makes about 12 tablespoons of paste
Preparation time: 15 minutes

16 small dried red chillies
1 tbsp coriander seeds
2 tsp cumin seeds
2 tsp white peppercorns (or black)
3 French shallots, sliced (or 1 small onion)
1 thumb-sized piece galangal (or ginger), peeled and roughly chopped

12 cloves of garlic, roughly chopped
2 tbsp sliced fresh or frozen lemongrass – pale part only
3 tsp grated Kaffir lime rind (or lime zest)
1 tbsp scraped, sliced coriander roots and stems
1 tsp shrimp paste
1 tsp sea salt

- Soak the chillies in hot water for about 10 minutes, drain and remove the seeds.
- Dry roast the coriander, cumin and peppercorns in a small hot pan, stirring and shaking the pan constantly to ensure they don't burn, for about a minute or until fragrant. Transfer immediately to a plate lined with kitchen paper and cool.
- Grind the spices to a fine powder in a mortar and pestle or electric coffee grinder.
- Combine all the ingredients except the ground spices in the bowl of a food processor, add a tablespoon or so of water and process until smooth. Or pound in a pestle and mortar until you have a smooth paste.
- Stir in the ground spices. Transfer the paste to a clean jar and refrigerate for up to a week or divide into 3 or 4 portions and freeze.

Green Curry Paste

This fresh, very hot curry paste is the only Thai paste that uses fresh rather than dried chillies. To make a paste that is not so hot, use the larger, milder green chillies and remove the seeds.

If you are making this paste using a pestle and mortar, use coarse sea salt as this helps to grind all the ingredients down.

Makes about 12 tablespoons of paste

2 tsp coriander seeds
1 tsp cumin seeds
2 tsp white peppercorns
20 fresh green Thai chillies (or a combination of mild and hot chillies)
10 cloves of garlic, roughly chopped
3 French shallots, sliced
1 thumb-sized piece of galangal (or ginger) peeled and roughly chopped

1 tbsp sliced fresh or frozen lemongrass, pale part only
2 tbsp sliced kaffir lime rind (or lime zest)
1 tbsp scraped, sliced coriander roots and stems
1 tsp shrimp paste
1 tsp sea salt

- Combine the coriander, cumin seeds and peppercorns in a small pan and roast over medium heat, stirring constantly for a minute or two, until aromatic. Immediately transfer to a plate lined with kitchen paper and cool.
- Grind the spices using an electric coffee grinder or pound in a pestle and mortar until finely ground.
- Combine all the ingredients except for the ground spices in the bowl of a food processor, add a tablespoon or two of water and process until smooth. Or pound in a pestle and mortar until you have a smooth paste.
- Stir in the ground spices. Transfer the paste to a clean jar and refrigerate for up to a week or divide into 3 or 4 portions and freeze.

Panang Curry Paste

This paste is spicier but not as hot as red or green curry paste. It is ideal for thicker textured curries such as the popular Panang curries.

Makes about 12 tablespoons of paste

5 long dried red chillies
1 tsp coriander seeds
½ tsp cumin seeds
1 tsp whole white peppercorns
2 cloves
1 cm (½ inch) piece of cinnamon
5 shallots or 1 large onion, sliced
10 cloves of garlic, peeled
2 tsp grated galangal or ginger

2 tsp sliced fresh or frozen lemongrass, white part only
1 tbsp scraped, sliced coriander roots and stems
1 tbsp grated Kaffir lime rind (or lime zest)
1 tbsp soft brown sugar
1 tsp sea salt
2 tsp shrimp paste

- Grind the chillies and spices to a fine powder using a coffee grinder or pestle and mortar. Set aside.
- Combine all the ingredients in the bowl of a food processor, add a tablespoon or two of water and process until smooth. Or pound in a pestle and mortar until you have a smooth paste.
- Transfer the paste to a clean jar and refrigerate for up to a week or divide into 3 or 4 portions and freeze.

Stocks

A good stock is invaluable for making really tasty soups and stews and the slow cooker makes preparing great stock really easy. It simmers everything very gently, allowing all the goodness and flavours to be leeched out of the bones and other ingredients, and because there's no evaporation you don't need to be around to watch the stock pot. Just put it on overnight or early morning and come home to the lovely aroma of flavoursome stock.

Chicken Stock

Good chicken stock is so easy to make, costs next to nothing and is essential for really tasty soups, sauces and curries.

Stock is best made on the Low setting.

Makes about 2 litres (3½ pints)
Preparation time: 5 minutes
Cook time: 8–10 minutes on Low

1–1½ kg (3 lb approximately) chicken bones
2.5 litres (4½ pints) cold water (approximately)
1 small onion, roughly chopped
½ stick celery, roughly chopped
½ carrot, roughly chopped
6 black peppercorns
2 bay leaves

- Rinse the bones in cold water, place in the slow cooker with all the remaining ingredients and switch on. Make sure there is enough water to cover, adding a little more if necessary. Cook for the stated time.
- Remove the lid and allow the stock to cool. Strain through muslin or a fine strainer into a clean container. Place in the fridge for several hours or overnight.
- Remove and discard the fat that will have set on top of the stock. It is now ready to use or you can freeze it for up to 3 months.

Recipe Notes:
- Your butcher should be able to give you some chicken carcasses. If not, buy a combination of chicken necks and wings.
- I tend not to add herbs and spices (or salt) to my stock so that I have a base that can be used for a lot of different dishes, but you can add sprigs of parsley, thyme, bay leaf and spices like cloves and cinnamon if you wish.
- This recipe was made in a 3.5 litre slow cooker. You can increase the quantities if you have a larger cooker.

Rich Beef Stock

This beef stock is so rich, meaty and delicious and yet so easy to make, you'll want to make it all the time. It's best made on the Low setting.

Makes about 2 litres (4½ pints)
Preparation time: 35 minutes
Cook time: 14 hours up to 24 hours on Low

1 stick celery, cut into large chunks
1 tsp peppercorns
2.5 litres (5½ pints) cold water
   (approximately)

1½ kg (3 lb approximately) meaty
   beef bones, cut into small pieces
1 tbsp tomato paste
1 onion, halved
1 carrot, cut into large chunks

- Preheat the oven to 220°C (425°F or Gas Mark 7). Meanwhile, place the celery, peppercorns and all but 1 cup of the water in the slow cooker and switch on.
- Place the beef bones in a roasting pan and brush with the tomato paste. Add the onion and carrot to the beef and roast for about 30 minutes.
- Remove the roasting pan from the oven and, using a slotted spoon, add the bones and vegetables to the slow cooker. Discard the fat in the pan and add the cup of water. Stir to dislodge the crusty bits sticking to the pan and add to the slow cooker.
- Ensure that all the ingredients are well covered with water, adding a little more if needed.
- After about 10 hours add more boiling water if needed. Do not stir.
- Remove the lid and allow the stock to cool. Strain through muslin or a fine strainer, into a clean container. Place in the fridge for several hours or overnight.
- Remove and discard the fat that will have set on top of the stock. It is now ready to use or freeze as required.

Recipe Notes:
- You can use any beef bones but try to get some with marrow in them such as leg bones.
- Ask your butcher to cut the bones into smallish pieces for you so that your stock will have the maximum flavour.

Vegetable Stock

Vegetable stock is often under-rated and viewed as a poor alternative to "real" stock used by those people who don't wish to consume anything meat based. A good vegetable stock, however, can hold its own against its meaty counterparts and there are indeed dishes, including non-vegetarian dishes, where only a vegetable stock will do.

A whole range of vegetables and vegetable trimmings can be used for making vegetable stock including tomatoes, mushrooms, parsnips, fennel and of course onions, carrots and celery. However, potato and the sulphurous vegetables like cauliflower and broccoli are not recommended.

Stock is best made on the Low setting.

Makes just over 2 litres (4½ pints)
Preparation time: 20 minutes
Cook time: 6–8 hours on Low

3 carrots, peeled and cut into large chunks
3 onions, quartered
2 stalks celery including leaves, cut into large chunks
1 small bulb of fennel, roughly chopped
1 bunch spring onions or a leek, white part only

2 cloves of garlic, peeled
1 tbsp good quality oil
1 fresh or dried bay leaf
1 tsp black peppercorns
2.5 litres (5½ pints) cold water (approximately)

- Combine the vegetables, garlic and oil in a heavy based saucepan and sweat on medium heat for about 5 minutes.
- Transfer the vegetables to the slow cooker, add the remaining ingredients and enough cold water to completely cover and switch the cooker on.
- Remove the lid and leave the stock to cool a little. Strain through a large sieve, pressing on the vegetables to extract as much flavour as possible.
- Cool completely and refrigerate the stock for up to 3 days, or freeze.

Meat Dishes

Thai Spiced Beef Soup

This is a really easy dish that is ideal for the slow cooker. It has wonderful, complex flavours that develop and get even better if the dish is left for a day before you eat it.

Serves: 5–6

Preparation time: 20 minutes

Cook time: 3–4 hours on High | 6–8 hours on Low

4 tbsp oil

1 kg (2¼ lb) blade or chuck steak, cut into 2.5 cm (1 inch) strips

2 cups (500 ml/18 fl oz) water

4 cups (1 litre/1¾ pints) beef stock (page 94)

4 tbsp red curry paste (page 89)

2 bay leaves

1 x 2.5 cm (1 inch) cinnamon stick

1 star anise

4 tbsp grated palm or soft brown sugar

4 tbsp soy sauce

4 tbsp fish sauce

Juice of 2 limes

2 cups shredded iceberg lettuce

3 cups bean sprouts

3 green onions, sliced

2 cups coriander leaves

To serve: rice or noodles, fish sauce and Hot and Sour sauce – stir 2 tablespoons of caster sugar into ½ cup of rice vinegar until dissolved; add 2 or more finely sliced chillies of choice.

- Heat half the oil in a wok or pan and brown the beef in two batches. Transfer to the slow cooker.
- Rinse the wok with the water and add to the beef with the stock, 1 tbsp of the curry paste, bay leaves, cinnamon, star anise and sugar. Stir well, cover and switch the slow cooker on to the desired setting.
- About 30 minutes before the end of cooking, heat the remaining oil in a wok or pan and fry the curry paste for 2–3 minutes until fragrant. Stir into the soup with the soy sauce, fish sauce and lime juice.
- Divide the lettuce and bean sprouts between serving bowls and serve the soup topped with the green onions and coriander leaves.

Thai Red Curry (with Beef)

This is a popular and easy recipe that produces a tasty and aromatic curry with lots of delicious sauce. It is just as good with lamb, pork or chicken.

Serves 4–5
Preparation time: 15 minutes
Cook time: 3–4 Hours on High | 6–8 Hours on Low

800 g (2 lb) blade or chuck steak, sliced into bite-sized pieces

2–3 kaffir lime leaves, torn (or two strips of lime rind)

2 lemon grass stalks, pale part only, bruised

400 ml (14 fl oz) can coconut milk

1 tsp salt

3 tbsp grated palm or soft brown sugar

2 tbsp oil

4 tbsp Thai red curry paste (page 89)

½ red capsicum, de-seeded and thinly sliced

½ green capsicum, de-seeded and thinly sliced

4 baby aubergines or 2 courgettes (zucchini) thickly sliced

½ cup sliced bamboo shoots (optional)

3 tbsp fish sauce or to taste

1 cup Thai (or sweet) basil leaves

1 mild red chilli, sliced for garnish

To serve: steamed jasmine rice, fish sauce, sliced chilli or hot sauce, lime wedges, chopped peanuts.

- Place the meat, lime leaves or rind and lemon grass in the slow cooker. Spoon off the thick coconut milk from the top of the can and set aside in the fridge.
- Add the remaining coconut milk, salt and sugar and add to the slow cooker. Add a little water if needed to just cover the meat. Cover and switch on to the desired setting.

- About 30 minutes before the end of cooking, heat the oil in a wok or pan and fry the curry paste for 2–3 minutes until fragrant.
- Add the reserved thick coconut milk and simmer for about 2 minutes. Add the vegetables and simmer for a further 3–4 minutes. Stir into the beef in the slow cooker and cook on High for the remaining time.
- Remove the lime leaves or rind and lemon grass. Add the fish sauce, taste and add more sugar or fish sauce if required.
- Stir through half the basil leaves and garnish with the remaining basil and sliced red chilli and serve.

Thai Green Curry (with Beef)

This creamy curry has a lovely fresh taste and aroma yet is incredibly easy to make. The curry can also be made with lamb, pork or chicken.

Serves 4–5
Preparation time: 15 minutes
Cook time: 3–4 Hours on High | 6–8 Hours on Low

800 g (2 lb) blade or chuck steak, sliced into bite-sized pieces
4 kaffir lime leaves, torn
400 ml (14 fl oz) coconut milk
1 tsp salt
3 tbsp grated palm or soft brown sugar
4 tbsp green curry paste

8 small Thai aubergines (or other aubergine), quartered
200 ml (7 fl oz) coconut cream
3 tbsp fish sauce (or to taste)
1 tbsp lime juice
½ cup coriander leaves
1 mild red chilli, sliced

To serve: steamed jasmine rice, fish sauce, sliced chilli or hot sauce, lime wedges.

- Place the beef and lime leaves in the slow cooker. Remove the thick coconut milk from the top of the can and set aside in the fridge.
- Add the remaining coconut milk, salt and sugar to the beef. Add a little water if needed to just cover the meat. Cover and switch the slow cooker on to the desired setting.
- About 30 minutes before the end of cooking, heat the reserved thick coconut milk in a wok or pan for 2–3 minutes. It will thin as it heats and then begin to thicken as it simmers.
- Add the curry paste and simmer for a further 2 minutes or until fragrant.
- Stir in the aubergine and sauté for 3–4 minutes. Stir in the coconut cream, heat through and add to the beef. Cook on High for 15–20 minutes.
- Stir in the lime juice. Add the fish sauce, taste and add more salt or sugar if needed. Serve garnished with coriander leaves and red chilli slices.

Massaman Curry

Massaman or Thai Muslim curry is quite unlike other typical Thai curries. The warm spices of the Indian subcontinent are combined with the fragrance of lemongrass, galangal and Kaffir lime making it quite unique. Massaman is a mild but aromatic, rich and hearty dish generally made with beef but it is just as good with pork, chicken or lamb.

Serves 4–5
Preparation time: 20 minutes
Cook time: 3–4 hours on High | 6–8 hours on Low

800 g (2 lb) stewing steak, sliced into 2.5 cm (1 inch) chunks
6 medium potatoes, peeled and quartered
3–4 kaffir lime leaves, finely shredded
2 bay leaves
6 cardamom pods
1 x 2.5 cm (1 inch) cinnamon stick
4 cloves
3 tbsp roasted peanuts, roughly chopped (optional)

5 tbsp red curry paste (page 89)
400 ml (14 fl oz) coconut milk
4 tbsp grated palm or soft brown sugar
1 tsp salt
2 tbsp oil
1½ cups (375 ml/12 fl oz) coconut cream
4 tbsp tamarind purée
3 tbsp fish sauce or to taste
2 tbsp lime juice

To serve: rice, roti, vegetable side dish, fish or soy sauce, sliced chilli or hot sauce.

- Place the meat, potatoes, kaffir lime leaves, bay leaves, spices and peanuts if using, into the slow cooker.
- Combine 1 tbsp of the curry paste with the coconut milk and add to the meat and potatoes. Sprinkle over the sugar and salt. Stir well, cover and switch the slow cooker on to the desired setting.
- About 45 minutes before the end of cooking, heat the oil and fry the curry paste over medium heat for 2–3 minutes until aromatic. Add the coconut cream and simmer for 3–4 minutes until thickened. Add to the slow cooker.
- Stir in the tamarind purée and fish sauce. Cook on the High setting for the remainder of the time, uncovered, stirring once or twice to allow the curry to thicken.
- Stir through the lime juice and taste. Add more sugar, and fish sauce if needed. Serve.

Beef Rendang

This delicious Malay dish can be described as a rich, flavourful and aromatic beef and coconut stew. Traditionally it is cooked long and slow until the meat is really tender and the sauce is so dry it clings to the juicy chunks of meat – ideal for the slow cooker.

Serves 4–5

Preparation time: 30 minutes

Cook time: 3–4 hours on High | 6–8 hours on Low

Rendang Paste

10 dried red chillies (soaked in warm water and de-seeded)

6 shallots or 1 large onion, peeled and roughly chopped

2 thumb-sized pieces of galangal or ginger, peeled and roughly chopped

3 stalks lemongrass (pale part only), roughly chopped

6–8 cloves of garlic

400 ml (14 fl oz) coconut milk

4 tbsp peanut, corn or sunflower oil

1 star anise

1 x 2.5 cm (1 inch) cinnamon stick

4 cardamom pods

800 g (2 lb) lean stewing beef, sliced into bite-sized pieces

1 tbsp tamarind purée

2 tsp salt or to taste

1 tbsp grated palm or soft brown sugar

1½ cups (375 ml/12 fl oz) hot water

6 tbsp desiccated coconut, lightly toasted

4 kaffir lime leaves, shredded

To serve: rice, vegetable side dish, lime wedges, fish or soy sauce.

- Pound or process the Rendang paste ingredients until finely chopped. Pour off the thick coconut milk from the top of the can and set aside.
- Heat the oil in a wok or pan and add the whole spices. Stir for 10 seconds and add the spice paste. Stir fry for 2–3 minutes until aromatic.

- Stir in the beef, tamarind, salt, sugar, the remaining liquid from the can of coconut milk and water. Stir and transfer to the slow cooker. Cover and switch the slow cooker on to the desired setting.
- About 45 minutes before the end of cooking add the reserved thick coconut milk, toasted coconut and shredded lime leaves and stir. Cook on High for the remaining time.
- Taste and add more sugar or salt as needed. Serve.

Recipe Notes:

• The whole spices are not meant to be eaten. Remove before serving or ask your diners to move them to the side of their plates.

• To toast coconut, heat a small non-stick pan over medium heat, add the coconut and stir continually until lightly browned. Remove from the pan immediately to stop the coconut from burning.

• Be careful when handling chillies. Wear rubber gloves or wash your hands carefully and do not touch your eyes.

Vietnamese Beef and Vegetable Stew

A tasty and aromatic dish, this is an easy, one-pot spicy stew that tastes even better the following day.

Serves 5–6
Preparation time: 30 minutes or less
Cook time: 3–4 hours on High | 6–8 hours on Low

3 tbsp oil
1 kg (2¼ lb) lean stewing steak, sliced into bite-sized pieces
2 carrots, cut into chunks
1 x 2.5 cm (1 inch) cinnamon stick
1 star anise
4 cloves
3 shallots or 1 large onion, thinly sliced
3–4 cloves of garlic, finely chopped
3 stalks lemon grass, pale part only, finely chopped
1 celery stalk, thinly sliced

1 cup diced fresh tomato or equivalent canned
1 tbsp grated palm or soft brown sugar
1 tsp salt
2 cups (500 ml/18 fl oz) beef stock or water
200 g (7 oz) green beans, topped and tailed and sliced in half crossways
2–3 hot green or red chillies, finely sliced
2 tbsp light soy sauce or to taste
½ cup sweet basil leaves, torn

To serve: rice, sliced chilli, soy sauce, lime wedges.

- Heat 1 tablespoon of the oil in a wok or pan and brown the beef well in two batches. Transfer to the slow cooker. Add the carrots, cinnamon, star anise and cloves.

- Heat the remaining oil in the same wok or pan and fry the shallots or onion for about 5 minutes until softened. Add the garlic, lemon grass and celery and fry for a further minute or two.
- Add the tomato, sugar and salt and cook until the tomato is pulpy. Add to the beef. Rinse the pan with the stock (or water) and add to the slow cooker. Add a little more water if required to just cover the meat and vegetables. Stir well, cover and switch the slow cooker on to the desired setting.
- About 30 minutes before the end of cooking, stir in the beans, chillies and soy sauce. Cook on High for the remaining time.
- Stir the basil leaves through just before serving.

Traditional Thai Pork Curry

This is a tasty, authentic curry with meat so juicy and tender it falls off the bone. It's an easy dish originating in northern Thailand. If time allows, cook it the day before to allow the delicious flavours to develop.

Serves 4–5

Preparation time: 20 minutes

Cook time: 3–4 hours on High | 6–8 hours on Low

1 kg (2¼ lb) trimmed pork shoulder, cut into large chunks
6 tbsp red curry paste (page 89)
3 tbsp oil
6 tbsp grated palm or soft brown sugar
6 cups (1.5 litres/2½ pints) hot vegetable stock or water
1 tbsp Thai curry powder or Indian curry powder (page 18)
3 tbsp roasted peanuts, roughly chopped
4 tbsp fish sauce
4 tbsp soy sauce
2 tbsp tamarind paste
1 thumb-sized piece of galangal or ginger, sliced into matchsticks (optional)
1 cup Thai basil leaves

To serve: rice, steamed greens, fish or soy sauce, sliced chilli, lime wedges.

- Combine the pork with a tablespoon of the curry paste. Heat a tablespoon of the oil in a wok or large pan and brown the meat in two or three batches and transfer to the slow cooker.
- Stir in the sugar and all but one cup of stock or water. Rinse the wok with the remaining stock or water and add to the meat. Cover and switch the slow cooker on to the desired setting.
- About 30 minutes before the end of cooking, heat the remaining oil in the wok or pan and fry the remaining paste and curry powder for 2 minutes or until aromatic.
- Stir in the peanuts, sauces and tamarind paste and stir the whole lot into the meat. Cook on High for the remaining time.
- Serve topped with the galangal (if using) and basil leaves.

Panang Curry

Panang curry is traditionally spicy but not hot. It is generally made with meat only, typically beef, and no vegetables are added. It's quite a dry curry with the thick sauce clinging to the meat. Pork, lamb and chicken are good alternatives if you want a change.

Serves 4–5

Preparation time: 20 minutes

Cook time: 3–4 hours on High | 6–8 hours on Low

800 g (2 lb) stewing steak, sliced into bite-sized pieces

4 tbsp Panang curry paste (page 91)

400 ml (14 fl oz) coconut milk

6 kaffir lime leaves, or 3 strips lime rind

1 cup (250 ml/8 fl oz) coconut cream

3 tbsp grated palm or soft brown sugar

½ cup ground roasted peanuts

4 tbsp fish sauce or to taste

1 mild red chilli, sliced

To serve: rice, roti, vegetable side dish, fish sauce, sliced chilli or hot sauce.

- Place the meat in the slow cooker. Combine 1 tbsp of curry paste with the coconut milk and add to the meat. Sprinkle over the kaffir lime or lime rind. Stir well, cover and switch on the slow cooker to the desired setting.
- About 45 minutes before the end of cooking, stir in the remaining curry paste, coconut cream, sugar, peanuts and fish sauce. Cook on High, uncovered, for the remaining time, stirring once or twice.
- Taste and add more fish sauce or sugar. Sprinkle over the red chilli before serving.

Sweet and Sour Curry with Pork

Sweet and sour flavours are popular with almost everyone and this dish of tender pork and vegetables is as colourful as it is delicious. As the meat is not coated in batter and deep fried, it is also healthy.

Chicken pieces with bone in are also good in place of the pork.

Serves 5–6
Preparation time: 40 minutes
Cook time: 2½–3½ hours on High | 5–7 hours on Low

4 tbsp peanut or sunflower oil
800 g (2 lb) trimmed pork loin, cut into 2.5 cm (1 inch) chunks
4 cloves of garlic, finely sliced
1 thumb-sized piece of ginger, finely sliced
1 x 2.5 cm (1 inch) cinnamon stick
1 tsp chilli powder or to taste
2½ tsp salt or to taste
3 cups (750 ml/1¼ pints) hot water
2 onions, thickly sliced
2 sticks celery, cut into chunks

1 small green capsicum, sliced
1 small red capsicum, sliced
2 tbsp curry powder (page 18)
1 orange, juiced
300 ml (10 fl oz) vinegar
4 tbsp tomato paste
6 tbsp soft brown sugar
2 cups pineapple chunks, fresh or canned
1½ tbsp cornflour dissolved in ½ cup of water
2–3 tbsp chopped fresh coriander

To serve: rice, sliced chilli or hot sauce, soy sauce.

- Heat a tablespoon of the oil in a wok or pan and brown the meat lightly, in two batches if necessary to avoid overcrowding, adding the garlic and ginger for the last 30 seconds or so. Transfer to the slow cooker.
- Add the cinnamon stick and sprinkle over the chilli powder and salt. Rinse the wok or pan with the water and add to the slow cooker. Stir well and add more water if required to just cover the meat. Cover and switch the slow cooker on to the desired setting.

- About 30 minutes before the end of cooking, heat the remaining oil and stir fry the onion, celery and capsicum for about 5 minutes over medium-high heat or until the onion just starts to colour.
- Stir in the curry powder and stir fry for about 30 seconds until aromatic. Add the orange juice and cook until about half of the liquid evaporates.
- Add the vinegar, let it bubble for a few seconds and stir in the tomato paste and sugar. Add to the curry together with the pineapple chunks and stir. Cook on High for the remaining time.
- Stir in the dissolved cornflour and cook, stirring gently, for 2–3 minutes until the sauce is thickened. Taste and add more sugar, vinegar or chilli if desired.
- Serve sprinkled with the coriander.

Vietnamese Beef Pho

It's hard to imagine a more nourishing and satisfying soup than this subtly spiced, delicious beef and noodle soup with fresh herbs. Pho (pronounced Fuh) is consumed widely throughout Vietnam and is really easy to make.

Serves 4–5

Preparation time: 30 minutes

Cook time: 5–6 hours on High | 10–12 hours on Low

Spiced Beef Broth

1 kg (2¼ lb) meaty beef bones

1 onion, roughly chopped

1 thumb-sized piece of ginger, thickly sliced

1 stalk lemon grass, pale part only, bruised

1 x 2.5 cm (1 inch) cinnamon stick

1 star anise

1 teaspoon black peppercorns

12 cups (3 litres/5 pints) hot water

1 tsp salt

400 g (14 oz) dried rice noodles or fresh or dried noodles of choice

2 cups bean sprouts

500 g (1 lb) beef fillet, very thinly sliced

To serve: 2 cups basil leaves, 2 cups mint leaves, 1 cup coriander leaves, sliced red or green chillies, 2 limes cut into wedges, fish sauce, hoisin sauce, chilli sauce.

- Wash the bones well, place in a large stock pot, cover with cold water and bring to the boil. Drain ensuring you get rid of all the foam. This helps ensure you get a clear broth.

- Place the bones in the slow cooker with all the broth ingredients except the salt. Cover and switch on to the desired setting. Cook for the appropriate time.
- Stir in the salt. Remove the bones and strain the broth. When ready to serve, bring the broth back to the boil and keep at a simmer.
- Soak the noodles in very hot water for 10 minutes or cook according to the packet instructions, drain and divide amongst serving bowls. Top with the bean sprouts and beef slices and pour the boiling hot broth over to cover.
- Serve with a platter of the herbs and garnishes and allow each diner to add fresh herbs, chillies and sauces according to taste.

Recipe Notes:

- To make this soup really authentic and if time allows, char the onion and ginger in a dry hot pan or under a hot grill for a few minutes before adding to slow cooker.
- To make it easier to thinly slice the beef, place it in the freezer for about 30 minutes or until it becomes firm.

Tamarind Pork

This is a tasty dish with hot, sour and salty flavours that requires relatively little preparation, perfect for those days when time is in short supply.

Serves 5–6
Preparation time: 20 minutes
Cook time: 3–4 hours on High | 6–8 hours on Low

3 large onions, coarsely chopped
6–8 cloves of garlic, coarsely chopped
5–6 tbsp peanut, sunflower or safflower oil
1 x 2.5 cm (1 inch) cinnamon stick
6 cloves
1 tsp turmeric

2 tsp salt
1 tsp shrimp paste
1.5 kg (3 lb) pork shoulder, cut into large chunks
3 tbsp tamarind purée
2 tbsp soy sauce
2 tsp crushed dried chilli or chilli powder
1 cup (250 ml/8 fl oz) hot water

To serve: rice, fish sauce, vegetable curry.

- Process the onion and garlic in a food processor or chop very finely.
- Heat the oil in a wok or large pan and add the cinnamon and cloves. Stir for about 10 seconds and add the onion mixture.
- Stir fry the onion on medium-high heat until quite brown, about 10 minutes. Add in the turmeric, salt and shrimp paste. Stir until incorporated.
- Add the pork and stir fry for about 2 minutes until the meat is sealed. Stir in the tamarind purée, soy sauce and chilli. Transfer to the slow cooker.
- Rinse the pan or wok with the water and add to the pork. Stir well, cover and switch the slow cooker on to the desired setting.
- If convenient, remove the lid for the final hour or so of cooking and cook on High, stirring now and again, to allow most of the moisture to evaporate. Alternatively, transfer the meat and juices to the wok or pan and stir fry on medium-high heat for 2 or 3 minutes. Serve.

Chicken Dishes

Malaysian Chicken Curry with Mango

Malaysian curries are heavily influenced by the curries of neighbouring countries like China and India, but the distinction is in the combination of tastes, textures and colours as demonstrated in this vibrant, delicious tasting dish.

Serves 4–5

Preparation time: 30 minutes or less

Cook time: 2½–3½ hours on High | 5–7 hours on Low

4 tbsp peanut, rice bran or sunflower oil

1 small green capsicum, thinly sliced

1 small red capsicum, thinly sliced

750 g (about 1¾ lb) chicken thigh fillets, sliced into bite-sized pieces

2 medium onions, minced

1 tbsp grated galangal or ginger

2 cloves of garlic, minced

1½ tsp salt or to taste

1 tbsp rice vinegar

3 tbsp grated palm or soft brown sugar

2½ cups (625 ml/20 fl oz) chicken stock or water

1 cup (250 ml/8 fl oz) coconut cream or thick coconut milk

1½ tbsp curry powder (page 18)

1 tbsp light soy sauce

2–3 ripe, fresh mangoes, peeled and sliced

To serve: rice, soy sauce, sliced chillies or hot sauce.

- Heat a tablespoon of oil in a wok or pan and stir fry the capsicums on medium heat for 5 minutes. Transfer to a plate and set aside in the fridge until required.
- Heat half the remaining oil in the same wok or pan and stir fry the chicken pieces, in two batches if necessary, until well sealed. Transfer to the slow cooker.

- Heat the remaining oil in the same pan and cook the onion, galangal and garlic over medium heat for about 5 minutes until softened. Stir in the salt, vinegar and sugar and add to the chicken in slow cooker.
- Rinse the pan with the stock or water and add to the slow cooker, cover and switch the slow cooker on to the desired setting.
- About 30 minutes before the end of cooking, stir through the capsicums, coconut cream or milk, curry powder and soy sauce.
- Add the mango just before serving, heat through and serve.

Curried Coconut Chicken

This is a simple but very tasty recipe with spicy Asian flavours balanced nicely with the sweetness of the sugar and coconut. Serve it with steamed rice and a vegetable stir-fry for a delicious and nutritious meal.

Serves: 5–6

Preparation time: 30 minutes or less

Cook time: 2½–3½ hours on High | 5–7 hours on Low

4 tbsp peanut, rice bran or sunflower oil

8 chicken thigh fillets, preferably free range, trimmed and each sliced into two pieces

1 onion, thinly sliced

3–4 cloves of garlic, thinly sliced

1 tsp chilli flakes

½ tsp turmeric

1 cup (250 ml/8 fl oz) puréed tomatoes, fresh or canned

3 tbsp tomato paste

2 cups (500 ml/18 fl oz) chicken stock or water

2 tbsp grated palm or soft brown sugar

2 tsp salt or to taste

1½ tbsp curry powder (page 18)

2 tbsp desiccated (unsweetened) coconut

1 cup (250 ml/8 fl oz) coconut cream or thick coconut milk

To serve: rice, vegetable side dish, sliced chillies or hot sauce.

- Heat half the oil in a wok or pan and brown the chicken pieces in two or three batches. Transfer to the slow cooker.
- Heat the remaining oil in the same wok or pan and fry the onion, garlic and chilli flakes for about 5 minutes or until the onion is softened. Stir in the turmeric and cook for a further few seconds.
- Add the tomatoes, paste, stock or water, sugar and salt and bring to the boil. Add to the chicken, stir well, cover and switch the slow cooker on to the desired setting.
- About 30 minutes before the end of cooking, stir through the curry powder, desiccated coconut and coconut cream or milk. Cook on High for the remaining time.

Burmese Chicken Curry

Burmese curries, though highly influenced by Indian cuisine, rarely contain the warm, aromatic spices that invariably flavour their Indian cousins. Large quantities of onions, garlic and ginger together with pungent belacan (shrimp paste) are used to add flavour. This is an easy dish that can be made with a whole chicken cut into serving size pieces or chicken thighs, drumsticks and wings as in this recipe.

Serves 5–6
Preparation time: 30 minutes
Cook time: 3–4 hours on High | 6–8 hours on Low

4 medium onions, roughly chopped
6–8 cloves of garlic, roughly chopped
2 thumb-sized pieces of ginger,
    roughly chopped
2 tsp shrimp paste
4 tbsp oil
1 tsp chilli powder or to taste

1.8 kg (4 lb) skinned chicken pieces –
    thighs with bone in, drumsticks
    and wings
1 cup (250 ml/8 fl oz) water
400 ml (14 fl oz) coconut milk
1½ tsp salt or to taste
1 tbsp light soy sauce or to taste
1 tbsp sesame oil (optional)
2–3 tbsp chopped fresh coriander

To serve: rice or noodles, vegetable side dish, soy sauce, sliced chilli, chilli flakes or hot sauce, lime or lemon wedges.

• Process the onion, garlic, ginger and shrimp paste until finely chopped. Heat the oil in a wok or large pan and fry the onion mixture for about 10 minutes on medium-high heat until lightly browned.

• Stir in the chilli powder and fry for a few seconds. Stir in the chicken pieces and stir until the chicken pieces are sealed. Transfer to the slow cooker.

• Rinse the wok or pan with the water and add to the slow cooker. Remove the thick coconut milk from the top of the can and set aside in the fridge.

• Add the remaining thin coconut milk to the chicken, stir in the salt, cover and switch the slow cooker on to the desired setting.

• About 30 minutes before the end of cooking stir in the thick coconut milk, soy sauce and sesame oil if using. Cook on High for the remaining time.

• Taste and adjust the seasoning, stir through the coriander and serve.

Vietnamese Chicken Pho

This version of chicken noodle soup would have to be amongst the tastiest and most comforting you can get. It's simple to make as long as you give it time, and with a slow cooker that is really easy.

Using chicken stock to make the spiced broth makes it wonderfully rich and flavoursome.

Serves 4–5
Preparation time: 30 minutes
Cook time: 8–10 hours on Low

Spiced Chicken Broth
1.5 kg (3 lb) chicken pieces (necks, drumsticks, wings) and bones
1 onion, roughly chopped
1 thumb-sized piece of ginger, thickly sliced
1 tbsp coriander seeds
1 stick cinnamon
1 star anise
1 tbsp sugar
10 cups (2.5 litres/4½ pints) chicken stock or water
1 tsp salt

2 chicken breast fillets (approximately 500 g/1 lb)
500 g (1 lb) dried rice noodles or fresh or dried noodles of choice
2 cups bean sprouts

To serve: 2 cups basil leaves, 2 cups mint leaves, 1 cup coriander leaves, sliced red or green chillies, sliced red onion, 2 limes cut into wedges, fish sauce, hoisin sauce, chilli sauce.

• Remove the skin and excess fat from the chicken pieces. Wash well and drain. Place in a large stock pot, cover with cold water and bring to the boil. Simmer for 2 or 3 minutes and drain.

- Rinse the chicken pieces again to remove all the scum and place in the slow cooker with the remaining broth ingredients. Cover and switch on to the desired setting.
- About 45 minutes before the end of cooking, add the breast fillets and cook on High for the remaining time or until the breast portions are cooked through.
- Remove the breast fillets and strain the broth through a fine sieve or muslin and discard the solids.
- When ready to serve, bring the broth back to the boil and keep hot. Shred the breast fillets using two forks, or slice thinly.
- Soak the noodles in very hot water for about 10 minutes or cook according to the packet instructions. Drain and divide amongst serving bowls. Top with the bean sprouts and shredded chicken and pour the hot broth over.
- Serve with a platter of herbs and garnishes and allow each diner to add fresh herbs, chillies and sauces according to taste.

Recipe Notes: To make this soup really authentic and if time allows, char the onion and ginger in a dry hot pan or under a hot grill for a few minutes before adding to the slow cooker.

Vietnamese Chicken and Vegetable Curry

A South Vietnamese style recipe, this dish is aromatic with fresh herbs and has a chilli hit that is nicely tempered by the sugar and coconut milk. It's easy to make, nutritious and very tasty.

Serves 5–6

Preparation time: 30 minutes

Cook time: 2½–3½ hours on High | 5–7 hours on Low

2–3 tbsp peanut, corn or sunflower oil

6 chicken thigh cutlets, bone in, skin removed

3 shallots or 1 medium onion, finely sliced

4–6 cloves of garlic, finely sliced

1 thumb-sized piece of ginger, julienned

2 stalks lemon grass, pale part only, finely sliced

1 tsp chilli flakes or to taste

400 ml (14 fl oz) coconut milk

2 cups (500 ml/18 fl oz) chicken or vegetable stock

2 carrots, diced

1 sweet potato, cut into 3 cm (just over 1 inch) chunks

1 tbsp grated palm or soft brown sugar

1 tsp salt

1 cup snow peas (mange tout)

1 tbsp curry powder (page 18)

3 tbsp fish sauce or soy sauce

½ cup sweet basil leaves

To serve: steamed rice, sliced chilli or hot sauce.

- Heat the oil in a wok or pan and add the chicken pieces. Stir fry for 2–3 minutes until lightly browned. Add the shallot or onion, garlic, ginger, lemon grass and chilli and stir fry for a further 3 minutes or so until aromatic. Transfer to the slow cooker.

- Pour off the thick coconut milk from the top of the can and set aside. Add the remaining coconut milk to the slow cooker. Rinse the wok or pan with the stock or water and add to the slow cooker.
- Add the carrot and sweet potato to the slow cooker, sprinkle over the sugar and salt, stir, cover and switch the slow cooker on to the desired setting.
- About 30 minutes before the end of cooking, stir the snow peas, curry powder and fish or soy sauce into the curry. Cover and cook on High for the remaining time.
- Garnish with the basil leaves just before serving.

Thai Chicken Soup in Coconut Milk

The flavour of this relatively simple soup will surprise you, it is really delicious. Yet it is so easy to prepare, despite the long list of ingredients. The use of dried ginger in the recipe is unusual but it gives this tasty soup an extra depth of flavour.

Serves 5–6
Preparation time: 20 minutes or less
Cook time: 2–3 hours on High | 4–6 hours on Low

2–3 chicken breast fillets (about 800 g/2 lb), trimmed
4 cups (1 litre/1¾ pints) chicken stock
½ onion, cut into 2 pieces
1 stick celery, cut into 3 pieces
2 stalks lemon grass, pale part only, bruised
4 kaffir lime leaves, torn
1 thumb-sized piece of galangal or ginger, grated
½ tsp dried ginger powder
3–4 cloves of garlic, finely sliced

1 tsp chilli flakes or to taste
2 carrots, thickly sliced
400 ml (14 fl oz) coconut milk
1 red capsicum, thinly sliced
1 cup fresh corn kernels (from 1 cob of corn)
1 cup baby green beans, topped and tailed
3 tbsp fish sauce (or salt) to taste
2 tbsp lime juice
½ cup coriander leaves
1 mild red chilli, sliced

To serve: jasmine rice, hot sauce made with 2 tbsp each of white vinegar and fish sauce with a sliced hot red chilli.

- Place the first 11 ingredients (up to and including the carrots) into the slow cooker. Cover and switch on to the desired setting.
- About 30 minutes before the end of cooking (or when the chicken is cooked), remove the chicken fillets and set aside. Remove the onion, celery and lemon grass and discard.

- Add the coconut milk, capsicum, corn and green beans to the slow cooker, cover and cook on High for about 20 minutes.
- Using two forks shred the chicken and return to the slow cooker with the fish sauce and lime juice. Heat through for about 5 minutes and taste. Add more fish sauce and lime juice if needed.
- Serve sprinkled with the coriander and chilli slices.

Indonesian Chicken Curry

Indonesian curries have evolved from Indian curries so there linger some distinct similarities but they have adjusted over time to suit Indonesian tastes and include local ingredients such as coconut milk, lemon grass and kaffir lime leaves for creamy, aromatic gravies.

Serves 4–5
Preparation time: 40 minutes or less
Cook time: 3–4 hours on High | 6–8 hours on Low

3 tbsp peanut or sunflower oil
3 shallots or 1 onion, finely sliced
1.8 kg (4 lb approximately) chicken, preferably free range, skinned and cut into serving size pieces
1 thumb-sized piece of ginger, finely sliced
3 cloves of garlic, finely sliced
1 tsp turmeric
1 x 2.5 cm (1 inch) cinnamon stick
4 cloves
6 cardamom pods

6 curry leaves (optional)
2 cups (500 ml/18 fl oz) hot water
2 tsp salt or to taste
1 tsp chilli powder or to taste
4 Kaffir lime leaves, shredded
1 stalk lemon grass, pale part only, bruised
1 tbsp curry powder (page 18)
1 cup (250 ml/8 fl oz) coconut cream
1 tbsp lime juice
1–2 tbsp coriander leaves

To serve: rice, vegetable dish, sliced chilli, lime wedges.

- Heat the oil in a wok or pan and fry the shallot or onion for about 5 minutes or until starting to brown at the edges.
- Add the chicken, ginger, garlic, turmeric, whole spices and curry leaves if using and stir fry on medium-high heat for 3–4 minutes or until the chicken is very lightly browned. Transfer to the slow cooker.
- Rinse the wok or pan with a little of the water and add to the slow cooker with the remaining water, salt, chilli powder, kaffir lime leaves and lemon grass, cover and switch on to the desired setting.
- About 30 minutes before the end of cooking, stir in the curry powder and coconut cream. Cook on High for the remaining time.
- Stir in the lime juice and serve sprinkled with the coriander.

Seafood Dishes and Vegetarian Dishes

Thai Seafood Curry

This is a tasty and satisfying fish and vegetable "stew" with delicious Thai flavours. It's easy to prepare and requires little more than steamed rice for a complete and nutritious meal. It is also good made with green curry paste instead of the red paste in the recipe and any combination of seafood you like.

Serves 6–7
Preparation time: 20 minutes
Cook time: 3–4 hours on High | 6–8 hours on Low

400 ml (14 fl oz) can coconut milk
3 tbsp red curry paste (page 89)
3 cups (750 ml/1¼ pints) chicken
   stock or vegetable stock
2 tbsp grated palm or soft brown
   sugar
1 thumb-sized piece of ginger,
   julienned
2 carrots, cut into small dice
3 cups shredded cabbage
1 cup frozen peas

2 tbsp oil
500 g (1 lb) white fish fillets, sliced
   into bite-sized pieces
250 g (½ lb) peeled fresh prawns
250 g (½ lb) scallops
3 tbsp fish sauce or to taste
½ cup (125 ml/4 fl oz) lime juice
½ cup Thai (or sweet) basil leaves
½ cup coriander leaves
1 mild red chilli, sliced

To serve: rice, fish or soy sauce, sliced chilli or hot sauce, lemon wedges.

- Pour off the thick coconut milk from the can and set aside.
- Combine the remaining coconut milk, 1 tbsp of the curry paste, stock and sugar and place in the slow cooker. Stir in the ginger, carrot and cabbage, cover and switch on the slow cooker to the desired setting.

- About 30 minutes before the end of cooking stir in the frozen peas and turn the slow cooker up to High setting.
- Heat the oil in a wok or pan and add the remaining curry paste. Stir fry for a minute and add the fish pieces and prawns. Cook stirring on medium heat for 2 minutes.
- Add the scallops and stir fry for a further minute or so. Transfer the seafood to the slow cooker.
- Add the reserved thick coconut milk to the wok or pan, stir and bring to a simmer. Stir in the fish sauce and add to the slow cooker. Cover and leave to cook for about 20 minutes or until the seafood is cooked through.
- Before serving, stir though the lime juice and basil leaves. Taste and add more fish sauce or sugar if needed. Serve garnished with the coriander and sliced chilli.

Thai Rice Soup with Prawns and Coriander

In many parts of Asia breakfast often takes the form of a rice soup put together from whatever is left over from the previous night's dinner simmered in a tasty stock. Referred to as Khao Tom in Thailand or Congee in China, it is (roughly translated) a kind of savoury rice porridge. This easy recipe is a freshly cooked version of this dish that I prefer to serve for lunch or dinner rather than breakfast and it is ideal for cooking in the slow cooker. I've been extravagant with the use of fresh king prawns but you can use chicken or pork for equally good results. Just slice the meat very thinly and add to the slow cooker together with the rice and other ingredients. It's great comfort food but also healthy and nutritious.

A good chicken stock is the key ingredient for a really tasty soup.

Serves 4–5

Preparation time: 15 minutes

Cook time: 2–3 hours on High | 4–6 hours on Low

8 cups (2 litres/3½ pints) chicken stock (recipe page 93)

1 cup jasmine rice

1 stalk lemongrass (pale part only) bruised

2 kaffir lime leaves (optional)

2 tsp minced or finely grated ginger or galangal

20 king prawns, shelled and de-veined, tails left intact

2–3 tbsp fish sauce to taste

1 cup coriander leaves

4 spring onions, trimmed and sliced into short lengths

To serve: Nam Pla Phrik (sliced red chilli in fish sauce), crispy fried onion, ground white or black pepper.

- Place the first four ingredients in the slow cooker, stir and switch on to the desired setting.
- About 30 minutes before the end of the cooking time, remove the lemongrass stalk and kaffir lime leaves if using, and stir in the ginger and prawns. Cook on High for the remaining time or until the prawns are cooked through.
- Before serving, stir through 2 tablespoons of fish sauce and do the taste test. Add a little more fish sauce if you wish, or serve extra at the table so each diner can add more if desired.
- Divide the prawns into deep bowls and ladle the soup over. Sprinkle on the coriander and spring onions and serve.

Thai Pumpkin Soup with Coriander

This is a delicious, beautifully spicy variation of a popular soup that's made extra special with an incredibly tasty, vibrant, fresh coriander sauce drizzled on top. Make it as mild or as spicy as you like.

Serves 6–7
Preparation time: 30 minutes
Cook time: 3–4 hours on High I 6–8 hours on Low

2 medium onions, sliced
1 thumb-sized piece of ginger, grated
3 tbsp red curry paste (page 89)
1 kg (2¼ lb) peeled pumpkin, cut into 2.5 cm (1 inch) chunks
5 cups (1.25 litres/2¼ pints) hot chicken or vegetable stock
2 tsp salt or to taste
2 tbsp grated palm or soft brown sugar
200 ml (7 fl oz) coconut cream

Red and green chillies, thinly sliced for garnish

Fresh Coriander Sauce
Bunch of coriander
Juice and zest of a lime
3–4 cloves of garlic, roughly chopped
1–2 hot green chillies, roughly chopped
2 tbsp fish sauce or ½ tsp salt

To serve: rice or crusty bread, hot sauce, fish or soy sauce.

- Combine the onion, ginger, curry paste, pumpkin, stock, salt and sugar in the slow cooker. Cover and switch on to the desired setting.
- Meanwhile, trim and discard the roots from the coriander and reserve some leaves for garnish. Process the remaining coriander with all the other sauce ingredients until smooth. Refrigerate until required.

- Blend the soup using a stick or jug blender and add a little hot water or stock if the soup is too thick.
- Stir in the coconut cream. Warm through for about 10 minutes on High. Taste and add more fish sauce or salt if required.
- Serve in bowls with the coriander sauce drizzled over the top and garnished with the sliced chillies and coriander leaves.

Sweet Potato, Coconut and Lime Soup

This smooth, creamy soup with typically Thai aromas and flavours is perfect for a cold winter's day. It's really easy to make and requires little preparation.

Preparation time: 20 minutes
Serves 6–7
Cook time 2–3 hours on High | 4–6 hours on Low

2 medium onions, sliced
2 tbsp red curry paste (page 89)
1 thumb-sized piece of galangal or ginger, grated
1 kg (2¼ lb) peeled sweet potato, cut into 2.5 cm (1 inch) chunks
6 cups (1.5 litres/2½ pints) chicken or vegetable stock

1 tsp salt
4 kaffir lime leaves, shredded
3 tbsp fish sauce or to taste
400 ml (14 fl oz) coconut cream
4 tbsp fresh lime juice
2 hot red chillies, de-seeded and finely chopped

To serve: rice or crusty bread, fish sauce, hot sauce, lime wedges.

- Combine the onion, curry paste, galangal or ginger, sweet potato, stock, salt and kaffir lime leaves in the slow cooker. Cover and switch on to the desired setting.
- When cooked, purée the soup using a stick or jug blender and add the fish sauce and about three-quarters of the coconut cream. Warm through for about 20 minutes on High.
- Stir through the lime juice and taste. Add more lime juice and fish sauce if needed. Serve with the remaining coconut cream swirled over the top and sprinkled with chilli.

9

North African and Other Spicy Dishes

THE CUISINES OF ASIA and the Indian sub-continent are not alone in celebrating the sheer magic of spices. A range of spices and spice blends are integral to the culinary cultures of many other parts of the world. Notably, Morocco in North Africa with its beautifully perfumed, honeyed tagines, the Caribbean with its pungent, peppery Jerk cooking, Mexico with its wonderful variety of chillies and South America with the robust flavours of its Creole and Cajun food all embracing their favoured spices in their own unique way. It always amazes me how the same ingredients can be transformed into so many wonderful flavours and aromas simply by the introduction of local influences and cooking techniques.

Aromatic Spice Blends

Ras-el-hanout

Ras-el-hanout is an exquisite, wonderfully fragrant blend of spices widely used throughout North Africa. A perfect example of how a large number of spices can be combined to create a beautifully harmonious mixture, the blend imparts a lovely golden colour as well as delicious flavours to almost every kind of food. It can be rubbed onto any kind of meat, fish or vegetable and stirred into rice and couscous.

In Arabic the name means "top of the shop" implying that Ras-el-hanout is the best of the best that a spice merchant has to offer. However, as is often the case with spice blends, there are as many recipes and variations as there are sellers and cooks but warm, aromatic spices like cinnamon, cardamom, cloves and nutmeg are generally included with other sometimes unusual ingredients such as hashish and spanish fly. My recipe doesn't contain ingredients quite that bizarre but does create a beautiful blend.

If there is an ingredient you can't get, just leave it out. Grind in small quantities to maintain optimum flavour and aroma, and store in an airtight container in a cool dark place for no longer than a month.

Makes about 2 tablespoons of Ras-el-hanout

2 tsp coriander seeds
1 tsp cumin
1 tsp fennel seeds
1 tsp allspice berries
½ tsp black peppercorns
½ tsp white peppercorns
6 cloves
6 green cardamom pods

2 brown cardamom pods, seeds only
½ nutmeg
1 x 2.5 cm (1 inch) cinnamon stick
1 tsp saffron strands
½ tsp cayenne
1 tsp turmeric
1 tsp ground ginger
1 tsp rock salt

- Combine all the ingredients and grind to a fine powder using a pestle and mortar or coffee grinder.

Zaataar (Za'taar)

Zaataar is the name for both a family of Middle Eastern herbs from the marjoram/oregano family and of the condiment combining these dried herbs with sesame seeds, salt and spices. Both the herb mixture and the condiment are used widely throughout the Middle East in a range of foods including meats, vegetables and breads. It is also delicious made into a paste with extra virgin olive oil and spread on fresh Lebanese style bread.

Western varieties of herbs do not have quite the same flavour and fragrance as the Middle Eastern varieties but the recipe below is close and amazingly aromatic and tasty. As with all spice blends, there are many variations so experiment with the quantities of ingredients until you get a blend you like best.

The traditional condiment is quite coarse so a pestle and mortar is ideal for grinding down the ingredients, but you can grind to a powder in a coffee grinder if you wish.

Makes just over a cup

½ cup of good quality dried savoury or thyme (or a combination)
1 tbsp dried oregano
1 tbsp dried marjoram
1 tbsp dried mint leaves

2 tbsp sumac berries (or ground sumac)
2 tbsp sesame seeds
1 tsp coarse salt

- Combine all the ingredients and grind as desired.

Harissa

Harissa is a fiery hot, garlicky Middle Eastern chilli paste which adds flavour to a whole range of foods. It can be stirred into soups, rice and couscous. It can be used for basting meat and fish, for flavouring marinades and salad dressings and even stirred into mayonnaise, yogurt or sour cream for a delicious dip. It's also easy to make.

I usually make this paste with dried red chillies because it keeps longer but it is just as good made with fresh chillies so use whichever you wish. You can also vary the type of chilli according to how hot you want the paste to be.

Makes about ¾ of a cup

About 40 (30 g/1 oz) dried red chillies
6 cloves of garlic, sliced
4 tbsp olive oil
2 tbsp lemon juice or red wine
    vinegar
½ tsp coarse salt
2 tsp ground coriander
1 tsp ground cumin

- Remove any stalks still attached to the chillies and soak in hot water for about half an hour or until soft. If the chillies are very full of seeds, remove about half.
- Combine the chillies with the garlic, olive oil, lemon juice or vinegar and salt and grind down to a paste using a pestle and mortar, blender or food processor.
- Stir in the spices and transfer to a clean airtight container. Drizzle on some extra oil and store in the fridge for up to 4 weeks if using dried chillies and up to a week if using fresh.

Note: Be careful when handling chillies, do not touch face or eyes and wash hands well afterwards. Or wear thin rubber gloves.

Jamaican Jerk Seasoning

Jamaican *Jerk* cooking is delicious. Like many cuisines it is a product of local and foreign influences – Asian, African, European and Indian. The method of seasoning and cooking food slowly in pits dug in the ground was brought to the Caribbean islands by African slaves. At the time, coating meat in spices was a way of preserving it, but the practice evolved to marinating and rubbing food with delicious spicy mixtures simply because people became hooked on the wonderful aromas and flavours that the spicy mixtures impart. It has become one the most popular ways of cooking food in the Caribbean.

The term Jerk refers to the method of cooking, the spice mixtures and the meat or fish that has undergone the seasoning and cooking process. There are many recipes for Jerk spice mixtures but the key ingredients are the very hot Scotch bonnet chillies, allspice and thyme. Additional spices like ginger, bay leaves, cinnamon, cloves and nutmeg are often included as are ingredients like brown sugar, soy sauce, tamarind, lime juice and rum or water.

The following recipe is for a dry spice mixture that can be combined with other dry and wet ingredients according to requirements. Whole spices ground in small quantities ensure the very best flavour and aroma.

Makes about ½ cup

6–8 dried Scotch bonnet, habanero or other hot chillies
1½ tbsp allspice berries
1 tbsp coriander seeds
1 tbsp white peppercorns
1 tsp yellow mustard seeds

6 cloves
½ nutmeg
2 tbsp dried thyme leaves
1 tsp rock salt
1 tbsp brown sugar

- Remove the stems from the chillies, combine all the ingredients and grind to a fine powder in a pestle and mortar or coffee grinder.
- Store the spices in an airtight container in a cool, dark place and use within 4–5 weeks for best results.

Meat and Poultry Dishes

Moroccan Lamb Tagine

This popular Moroccan dish has a lovely depth of spicy and slightly sweet flavours and the meat is falling-off-the-bone tender. Serve it with a vegetable side dish, or add more vegetables and/or chickpeas to turn it into a complete one-pot meal.

There should be lots of deeply tasty sauce and it is traditionally quite thin, making it perfect to eat with couscous.

Serves 4–5

Preparation time: 30 minutes or less

Cook time: 3–4 hours on High | 8–9 hours on Low

Tagine Spice Mix
2 tsp dried ground ginger
2 tsp paprika
½ tsp ground turmeric
1 tsp ground cumin
1 tsp ground coriander
½ tsp cayenne pepper

1 kg (2¼ lb) lamb with bone in, cut into large pieces
3 tbsp good quality oil
2 medium onions, thinly sliced
3–4 cloves of garlic, finely sliced

3 cups (750 ml/1¼ pints) hot water
2 x 2.5 cm (1 inch) cinnamon sticks
4 green cardamom pods
4 cloves
2 carrots, peeled and diced
1 tsp salt (or to taste)
2 pieces orange peel about 2 cm
    (1 inch) wide and about 7 cm
    (3 inches) long
6 prunes, chopped in 3 or 4 pieces
Juice of 1 orange
2 tsp honey
Pinch saffron (optional)

To serve: couscous, harissa (page 137), salad.

- Place the lamb in a bowl or other non-corrosive container, add 1 tablespoon of the oil and sprinkle over half the spice mix. Mix until all the pieces are well coated with the spice and oil. Cover and set aside.

- Heat the remaining oil in a wok or pan and sauté the onion and garlic for about 5 minutes or until softened. Remove from the pan and place in the slow cooker.
- Heat the pan again and brown the meat well in two or three batches. Add a little more oil if required. Place the meat on top of the onion.
- Rinse the pan with a little of the water and add to the meat and onion with the remaining water.
- Stir in the whole spices, carrots, salt and orange peel. Push everything down into the liquid to ensure all the pieces are immersed. Add a little more water if needed and cook on the desired setting.
- About 30 minutes before the end of the cooking time, add the remaining spice mix, prunes, orange juice, honey and saffron if using, and stir into the tagine. Cook on High for the remaining time.

Chicken Tagine with Preserved Lemon

This is another popular Moroccan dish bursting with complex flavours. There are many variations to the basic recipe but the saffron, ginger and pepper are typically used in all traditional recipes.

Serves 4–5

Preparation time: 40 minutes or less

Cook time: 3–3½ hours on High | 6–7 hours on Low

2 cloves of garlic, ground to a paste
¼ tsp freshly ground black pepper
4 tbsp olive or other good quality oil
1.5 kg (3 lb approximately) chicken, preferably free range, skinned and cut into serving sized pieces
2 medium onions, finely chopped
½ tsp turmeric
½ tsp ground ginger
2 tsp salt or to taste

1 stick cinnamon
2 bay leaves, fresh or dried
3 cups (750 ml/1¼ pints) hot water
½ tsp saffron threads, soaked in a little warm water
½ tsp ground cumin
1 tsp ground coriander
1 tsp paprika
1 cup green olives
1 preserved lemon, thinly sliced

To serve: couscous, harissa (page 137), salad.

- Combine the garlic and black pepper with about half the oil and rub over the chicken pieces.
- Heat a wok or pan over high heat and brown the chicken pieces lightly, in two batches if necessary. Transfer to the slow cooker.
- Heat the remaining oil in the same wok or pan and fry the onion for about 5 minutes until starting to brown. Stir in the turmeric, ginger and salt and add to the chicken together with the cinnamon stick and bay leaves.
- Rinse the wok with a little of the water and add to the slow cooker with the remaining water. Stir well, cover and switch on to the desired setting.
- About half an hour before the end of cooking, stir in all the remaining ingredients. Cook on High for the remaining time.

Moroccan Beef and Vegetable Stew

Although the list of ingredients seems quite long this is an easy dish to prepare and it is really delicious – juicy, tender chunks of meat and tasty vegetables in an aromatic, sweetly spiced broth.

Serves 5–6

Preparation time: 30 minutes

Cook time: 3–4 hours on High | 6–8 hours on Low

4 tbsp olive or other good quality oil
800 g (2 lb) blade or stewing steak, sliced into bite-sized pieces
2 medium onions, thinly sliced
1–2 cloves of garlic, finely chopped
2 x 2.5 cm (1 inch) cinnamon sticks
1 tsp turmeric
1 tsp ground ginger
3 cups (750 ml/1¼ pints) hot water
2 cups (500 ml/18 fl oz) beef stock

1 medium sweet potato, cut into large (about 4 cm) chunks
2 carrots, sliced into 1 cm (½ inch) rings
2 tsp salt or to taste
1 tsp cayenne or chilli powder
1 cup apricots, quartered
½ cup sultanas
2 tbsp honey
1 tsp orange zest

To serve: couscous, harissa (page 137), salad.

- Heat a tablespoon of oil in a wok or pan and brown the steak lightly. Transfer to the slow cooker.
- Heat the remaining oil in the same wok or pan and fry the onion, garlic and cinnamon for 4–5 minutes over medium-high heat until the onion is soft and starting to brown at the edges.
- Stir in the turmeric and ginger, stir once and add to the meat in the slow cooker. Rinse the wok or pan with a little of the water and add to the slow cooker with the remaining water and stock.
- Add the sweet potato, carrot, salt, cayenne, apricots and sultanas. Stir, cover and switch the slow cooker on to the desired setting.
- About 20 minutes before the end of cooking, stir in the honey and orange zest. Let the dish stand for about 10 minutes before serving.

Moroccan Lamb Soup

Referred to as Harira, this fragrant, hearty soup is loved by Moroccans particularly during the month of Ramadan when it is often eaten to break the fast at sunset. Recipes vary from household to household. Some cooks like to make it light in texture while others add vermicelli and chickpeas to make it into a more filling meal, so vary it according to your own preference.

Serves 5–6
Preparation time: 40 minutes or less
Cook time: 2½–3½ hours on High | 5–7 hours on Low

3 tbsp olive oil
500 g (1 lb) lean lamb, diced
2 medium onions, finely chopped
2 cloves of garlic, finely chopped
2 celery stalks with leaves, finely chopped
2 x 2.5 cm (1 inch) cinnamon sticks
½ tsp turmeric
3 tsp ground ginger
3 tsp salt or to taste
½ tsp cayenne pepper (optional)
750 g (1½ lb) ripe tomatoes, puréed (or equivalent amount bottled passata)

½ cup green or brown lentils, picked for stones, rinsed and drained
8 cups (2 litres/3½ pints) lamb or beef stock
90 g (3 oz) vermicelli or spaghetti, broken into short lengths
1 tsp freshly ground black pepper
¼ cup finely chopped parsley
1 tbsp cornflour dissolved in ½ cup water
2 tbsp grated Parmesan (optional)
¼ cup finely chopped fresh coriander

To serve: harissa (page 137), lemon wedges, salt and pepper, flat or crusty bread.

- Heat a tablespoon of the oil in a wok or pan and brown the lamb well over medium-high heat for 2 or 3 minutes. Transfer to the slow cooker.

- Heat the remaining oil in the same wok or pan and sauté the onion, garlic, celery and cinnamon over medium heat for about 3–4 minutes until the onion is softened.
- Stir in the turmeric, ginger, salt and cayenne if using. Stir once and add the puréed tomatoes. Bring to a simmer and add to the slow cooker with the lentils.
- Rinse the wok or pan with a little of the stock and add to the slow cooker with the remaining stock. Stir well, cover and switch on to the desired setting.
- About 30 minutes before the end of cooking stir in the pasta, pepper and chopped parsley. Cook on High for the remaining time.
- Keeping the setting on High, stir through just over half the cornflour and water. Simmer for 2 or 3 minutes, stirring once or twice until the soup is thickened and no longer cloudy. Add more cornflour if you want the soup thicker.
- Stir in the Parmesan and coriander just before serving.

Moroccan Chicken and Chickpea Stew

This is a delicious but easy recipe with chicken pieces gently cooked until really tender in a fragrantly spiced sauce with chickpeas and apricots. Prunes, sultanas or raisins can be used instead of apricots if preferred.

Serves: 4–5

Preparation time: 30 minutes or less

Cook time: 2½–3½ hours on High | 5–7 hours on Low

3 tbsp oil

1.5 kg (3 lb) chicken, preferably free range, skinned and cut into serving size portions

1 onion, thinly sliced

1 carrot, diced

1 x 2.5 cm (1 inch) cinnamon stick

2 whole cloves

1 bay leaf

2 cloves of garlic, finely chopped

½ tsp turmeric

2 tsp salt or to taste

3 ripe tomatoes, diced

½ tsp cayenne or chilli powder

4 cups (1 litre/1¾ pints) chicken stock or water

1 cup chickpeas soaked overnight (or 1 x 400 g/14 oz can), drained

6 dried apricots, chopped

1 orange, juiced

1 tsp freshly ground black pepper

Pinch of saffron threads soaked in ¼ cup hot water (optional)

1 tbsp Ras-el-hanout (page 135) or curry powder (page 18)

1 tbsp chopped parsley

1 tbsp chopped fresh coriander

To serve: couscous, harissa (page 137), flat bread.

- Heat a tablespoon of oil in a wok or pan and brown the chicken pieces lightly. Transfer to the slow cooker.
- Heat the remaining oil in the same wok or pan and fry the onion, carrot, cinnamon, cloves and bay leaf over medium heat for about 5

minutes or until the onion has softened. Add the garlic and fry until aromatic, about a minute.

- Stir in the turmeric and salt, stir once and add the tomatoes. Cook over medium to high heat for 2 minutes or until the tomatoes are pulpy. Stir in the cayenne or chilli powder and add to the chicken in the slow cooker.
- Rinse the wok or pan with a little of the stock and add to the slow cooker with the remaining stock. Stir in the chickpeas and apricots, cover and switch on to the desired setting.
- About 30 minutes before the end of cooking, stir in the orange juice, black pepper, saffron, Ras-el-hanout or curry powder and parsley. Cook on High for the remaining time.
- Stir in the coriander just before serving.

Brown Rice Jambalaya

There are so many recipes and varieties of Jambalaya that it is said that, like the Italian puttanesca, if you have it in the pantry you can put it in the pot. The main ingredients in traditional recipes are rice, meat, spicy smoked sausage and seafood flavoured with dried herbs and cayenne pepper. The traditional way of cooking it is long and slow so a slow cooker is ideal for making great jambalaya.

The highly smoky Cajun andouille sausage is wonderful in this dish but the French andouille is a good substitute or use any other spicy smoked sausage.

Serves 6–7
Preparation time: 30 minutes or less
Cook time: 3–4 hours on High | 6–8 hours on Low

Cajun spice mix
1 tbsp paprika
½ tsp garlic powder
½ tsp ground white pepper
½ tsp ground black pepper
1 tsp cayenne pepper (or to taste)
½ tsp dried thyme
1 tsp dried oregano

4 tbsp olive oil
450 g (1 lb) spicy smoked sausage,
    sliced into 2.5 cm (1 inch) lengths
750 g (1½ lb) chicken wings and
    drumsticks, skinned if preferred

1 onion, finely chopped
2 sticks celery, thinly sliced
1 green or yellow capsicum, diced
2 carrots, diced
2 tsp turmeric
4 cups (1 litre/1¾ pints) chicken stock
2 cups brown or Arborio rice, rinsed
    and drained
2 tsp salt or to taste
2 cups frozen peas
450 g (1 lb) peeled prawns

- Heat a tablespoon of oil in a wok or pan and brown the sausage over medium heat. Transfer to the slow cooker.
- Add another tablespoon of oil to the same wok or pan and brown the chicken pieces lightly. Add to the sausage in the slow cooker.

- Heat the remaining oil and sauté the onion, celery, capsicum and carrots over medium heat for about 5 minutes until softened. Stir in the turmeric and spice mix and cook for a few seconds. Add to the slow cooker.
- Rinse the wok or pan with a little of the stock and add to the slow cooker with the remaining stock, rice and salt. Stir well, cover and switch the slow cooker on to the desired setting.
- About 30 minutes before the end of cooking stir in the peas and prawns. Cook on High for the remaining time until the prawns are cooked through.
- Let the jambalaya stand for about 5 minutes before serving.

Real Chilli Con Carne

Chilli con Carne originates in Texas and Texans believe that no one makes it as well as they do. The original chilli was concocted by native Indians using tough, old goat meat with enough spice added to disguise the terrible taste of the meat but the modern chilli is made using flavoursome, stewing cuts of beef with or without beans and just enough chilli powder to provide a robust chilli hit.

Serves 4–5
Preparation time: 30 minutes or less
Cook time: 4–5 hours on High | 8–10 hours on Low

1 tbsp cumin seeds
2 tbsp olive oil
2 ancho chillies, de-seeded and crushed or 1 tsp chilli flakes
1 tsp chilli powder or to taste
1 kg (2¼ lb) stewing steak, trimmed and cut into 1 cm (just under ½ inch) dice
2 medium onions, finely sliced

2–3 cloves of garlic, finely chopped
6 ripe tomatoes, diced (or equivalent canned)
2 tsp salt or to taste
1½ cups (375 ml/12 fl oz) water (approximately)
1 x 400 g (14 oz) can kidney beans or chickpeas, drained (optional)

To serve: rice, salad.

- Crush the cumin seeds lightly using a pestle and mortar. Heat a wok or pan on medium heat and dry fry the cumin for about 30 seconds or until aromatic.
- Add the oil, crushed ancho chilli or chilli flakes and chilli powder and cook over medium heat for about a minute.
- Add the meat and turn up the heat. Brown the meat well for about 3 minutes. Add the onion and garlic and stir fry for a further minute.

Stir in the tomatoes and salt, bring to a simmer and transfer to the slow cooker.

- Rinse the pan with the water and add to the meat. Cover and switch on to the desired setting.
- About 30 minutes before the end of cooking, stir in the beans or chickpeas if using. Finish cooking on High.
- Taste and add more chilli if desired. Cool and refrigerate for 24 hours (if possible) to let the flavours develop and re-heat gently before eating.

Recipe Notes:

- If the chilli is too thin, thicken it using a teaspoon or so of cornflour dissolved in a tablespoon of cold water. Simmer, stirring constantly, for 2–3 minutes to cook the cornflour. Remember, it will thicken further on cooling.
- If you don't wish to use beans, increase the quantity of meat by about the same amount.

Slow Cooked Jamaican Jerk Chicken

This is an easy recipe for a robustly spiced delicious chicken dish. The rum gives it the "oomph" factor so do use it if you can. Jerk Chicken is best eaten the day it is cooked.

Serves 4–5
Preparation time: 30 minutes or less
Cook time: 3–4 hours on High | 6–8 hours on Low

1½ tbsp Jamaican Jerk Seasoning (page 138)
1.8 kg (4 lb approximately) chicken, preferably free range, skinned and chopped into serving sized pieces or thighs and drumsticks
3 tbsp olive oil
2 medium onions, roughly chopped
1 thumb-sized piece of ginger, roughly chopped
3–4 cloves of garlic, roughly chopped
2 tbsp Jamaican rum
2 tbsp red wine vinegar
1 orange juiced
3 tbsp soy sauce or to taste
1 tbsp molasses or dark brown sugar

To serve: Jamaican rice and peas (page 175) or plain rice and a vegetable side dish.

- Sprinkle the seasoning over the chicken pieces, add the oil and mix well. Set aside.
- Combine all the remaining ingredients in a blender jug and blend until you have a smooth purée.
- Heat a wok or pan and brown the chicken pieces well. Transfer to the slow cooker and pour over the onion mixture.
- Mix well, cover and switch on to the desired setting.
- Taste for seasoning and add a little more soy sauce if required. Let the dish stand for about 10 minutes and serve.

Jamaican Pork and Potato Curry

A really tasty and satisfying, easy-to-cook curry that is just as good made with chicken. The dish is best served on the day it is cooked.

Serves 4–5
Preparation time: 30 minutes or less (plus marinating time)
Cook time: 3–3½ hours on High | 6–7 hours on Low

800 g (2 lb) pork shoulder, cut into 4 cm (just under 2 inches) chunks
1 small red capsicum, sliced
1½ tbsp Jamaican Jerk Seasoning (page 138) or Jamaican curry powder
1 tsp turmeric
2 tsp mustard powder
2 medium onions, finely chopped
1 thumb-sized piece of ginger, finely chopped

3–4 cloves of garlic, finely chopped
3 tbsp soy sauce or to taste
2 tbsp lime juice or red wine vinegar
2 tsp soft brown sugar
2 tbsp olive oil
3 medium potatoes, peeled and quartered
1½ cups (375 ml/12 fl oz) hot water
1 tsp salt or to taste
1 or 2 fresh Scotch bonnet, habanero or other hot chilli, finely chopped

To serve: rice, roti.

- Place the pork and capsicum in a medium non-corrosive bowl and sprinkle over the seasoning or curry powder, turmeric and mustard powder.
- Combine the onion, ginger, garlic, soy sauce, lime juice or vinegar and sugar in the bowl of a food processor and process until fine.
- Add to the pork, mix well, cover and place in the fridge to marinate for at least 2 hours or overnight if time allows. Remove from the fridge about half an hour before cooking to allow the meat to return to room temperature.
- Heat the oil in a wok or large pan and brown the pork mixture well (in two or three batches if necessary) for about 5 minutes. Transfer to the slow cooker and add the potatoes.
- Rinse the pan with the water and add to the slow cooker. Stir in the salt, cover and switch the slow cooker on to the desired setting.
- Stir through the chilli about half an hour before serving.

Fajitas with Mexican Barbacoa

If you like Mexican food in general and Fajitas in particular, you'll love this recipe.

Traditional Mexican barbacoa or barbecue generally refers to large pieces of meat, sometimes whole sheep, covered with banana leaves and steamed over a large pot of water in a fire pit dug in the open ground. I'm happy to say that the process below is much easier than this but still produces great results with the slow cooker adequately replicating the moist cooking heat of the fire pit.

Deboned lamb shoulder cut into large chunks or beef cheeks are both good so use whichever you prefer. Leaner cuts are not suitable as the meat dries out too much.

Serves: 6–8
Preparation time: 30 minutes or less
Cook time: 6–7 hours on High

1 tbsp cumin seeds
2 tsp salt
1.5 kg (3 lb) lamb shoulder or beef cheeks
2 tbsp oil
2 medium onions, sliced
1 whole head of garlic, separated into cloves and peeled

2 bay leaves
1 tbsp oregano
1 cup (250 ml/8 fl oz) cider vinegar
4 smoked ancho chillies (optional)
2 chipotle chillies, ground (optional)

To serve: corn or flour tortillas, salsa, guacamole, sour cream, sliced red onion, shredded lettuce, lime wedges, sliced pickled jalapenos, hot sauce.

- Heat a large, heavy based frying pan and toast the cumin seeds for a few seconds until aromatic. Remove from the pan immediately to prevent burning and transfer to the slow cooker.

- Rub the salt over the meat. Heat a tablespoon of oil in the same pan and brown the meat well in two or three batches. Don't overcrowd the pan or the meat will stew rather than brown. Transfer to the slow cooker.
- Heat the remaining oil until very hot and cook the onion and garlic until lightly charred. Add to the slow cooker with all the other ingredients. Turn the meat over in the liquid until each piece is well coated. Cover and switch the slow cooker on to High setting.
- After about 3 hours, turn the meat pieces around in the juices again. Repeat after about 1½ hours and let it cook for another 1½ hours. The meat should be falling apart after this time but, if not, cook for another hour or so.
- Drain the meat from the juices. Let it stand for a few minutes and shred using two forks. Drizzle a little of the meat juices over to moisten. Serve.

Chicken Chow Mein

This slow cooked version of the popular Chinese dish is nutritious and tasty and is likely to please just about everyone. Slow cooking really brings out the flavour and aroma of all the vegetables.

Serves 5–6
Preparation time: 30 minutes
Cook time 2½–3½ hours on High | 5–7 hours on Low

2 tbsp peanut or sunflower oil
6 chicken thigh fillets, cut into 2.5 cm (1 inch) chunks
1 large thumb-sized piece of ginger, thinly sliced
3 cloves of garlic, finely sliced
10 spring onions, white and pale part sliced, green shoots reserved
3 carrots, thinly sliced
3 stalks celery, thickly sliced
2 cups (500 ml/18 fl oz) chicken stock (page 93)

1 tbsp sugar
1½ tbsp cornflour dissolved in ½ cup water
1 x 200 g (7 oz) can water chestnuts, drained (and sliced if preferred)
2 cups bean sprouts
1 or 2 red chillies, finely sliced
1/3 cup (80 ml/3 fl oz) light soy sauce
150g (5 oz) dried crunchy chow mein noodles

To serve: rice or soft noodles, soy sauce, lime wedges, sliced red chilli, hot sauce.

- Heat 1 tbsp of the oil in a wok or large pan and lightly brown the chicken pieces in two batches. Transfer to the slow cooker.
- Heat the remaining oil and lightly sauté the ginger, garlic, white part of the spring onion, carrots and celery for about 3 minutes. Add to the slow cooker.
- Rinse the wok or pan with a little of the stock and add to the cooker with the remaining stock and sugar. Cover and switch on to the desired setting.

- About 20 minutes before the end of cooking, stir in just over half the cornflour. Cook, stirring, on High for about 3 minutes or until the mixture is no longer cloudy. Add more cornflour if you want a thicker sauce.
- Holding all the reserved green spring onion shoots in a bunch, slice two lots of 5 cm (2 inch) lengths from the cut ends, discarding the remainder. Add to the slow cooker with the water chestnuts, bean sprouts, chillies and soy sauce. Heat through for 5 minutes and serve topped with the crunchy noodles.

Vegetable Dishes

Moroccan Chickpea and Lentil Soup

A tasty and substantial vegetarian dish, this is really easy to make. Whilst good on its own, this soup can also be served as a side dish with a meat curry.

Serves 4–5 as a main dish, more as a side dish
Preparation time: 30 minutes or less
Cook time: 3–4 hours on High | 6–8 hours on Low

2 onions, roughly chopped
2 cloves of garlic, roughly chopped
Small knob of ginger, roughly chopped
2 tbsp olive oil
1 stick of celery, thinly sliced
1 carrot, diced
3 ripe tomatoes, diced
1 tbsp curry powder (page 18)
2 tsp salt or to taste

8 cups (2 litres/3½ pints) hot water
1 cup brown lentils, picked over, rinsed and drained
1 cup chickpeas soaked overnight, drained
Pinch saffron threads (optional)
1 green chilli, finely sliced
2 tbsp chopped parsley
2 tbsp chopped fresh coriander

To serve: harissa (page 137), couscous, rice or flat bread.

- Combine the onion, garlic and ginger in the bowl of a food processor and process until finely chopped.
- Heat the oil in a wok or pan and add the onion mixture, celery and carrot and sauté for 3–4 minutes.
- Add the tomato, a teaspoon of the curry powder and the salt. Cook for a couple of minutes and add about 2 cups of the water. Transfer to the slow cooker with the remaining water, lentils and chickpeas. Cover and switch on to the desired setting.
- About 30 minutes before the end of cooking stir in the remaining curry powder, saffron if using, chilli and parsley.
- Stir through the coriander and serve with harissa, allowing each diner to stir the condiment through the soup according to personal taste.

Vegetable Tagine

This fragrant and spicy vegetarian tagine is easy to prepare and a great meat-free meal or a tasty side dish to a meat tagine.

Serves 4–5 as a main dish, more as a side dish
Preparation time: 30 minutes or less
Cook time: 3–4 hours on High | 6–8 hours on Low

3 tbsp olive oil
2 medium onions, sliced
2 cloves of garlic, finely sliced
Small knob of ginger, grated
1 x 2.5 cm (1 inch) cinnamon stick
1 tsp turmeric
2 tsp salt or to taste
3 cups (750 ml/1¼ pints) hot water
1 tsp cayenne or chilli powder to taste
4 carrots, cut into sticks

2 medium potatoes, quartered
1 cup chickpeas, soaked overnight
   and drained
2 tbsp chopped dried apricots, golden
   raisins, or prunes
1 tbsp Ras-el-hanout (page 135) or
   curry powder (page 18)
1 tbsp honey
½ tsp freshly ground black pepper
2 tbsp chopped fresh coriander

To serve: rice, couscous or flat bread, harissa (page 137), yogurt.

- Heat the oil in a wok or pan and fry the onion for 3–4 minutes until starting to brown at the edges. Add the garlic, ginger and cinnamon and cook for 1–2 minutes until aromatic.
- Stir in the turmeric, stir once and add the salt and about half the hot water. Transfer to the slow cooker.

- Rinse the wok or pan with the remaining water and add to the slow cooker with cayenne or chilli powder, carrots, potatoes, chickpeas and fruit. Stir well, cover and switch the slow cooker on to the desired setting.
- About 30 minutes before the end of cooking stir in the Ras-el-hanout or curry powder, honey and black pepper.
- Stir through the coriander just before serving.

Moroccan Cauliflower and Potato Curry

This is a really simple dish with subtle spicy flavours. Add a little more cayenne if you want to spice it up a bit and a can of chickpeas if you want a more substantial meal.

Serves 4–5 as a main dish, more as a side dish
Preparation time: 30 minutes
Cook time: 2–3 hours on High | 4–6 hours on Low

3 tbsp olive oil
2 medium onions, finely sliced
1 x 2.5 cm (1 inch) cinnamon stick
1 tsp fennel seeds
½ tsp cayenne or chilli powder
2 tsp salt or to taste
1 tsp turmeric
2 carrots, sliced

3 medium potatoes, cut into 2 cm
   (just under 1 inch) chunks
1 tbsp tomato paste
2½ cups (625 ml/20 fl oz) hot water
1 small head cauliflower (about
   800 g/2 lb), cut into large florets
1 tbsp curry powder (page 18)
1 cup frozen peas

To serve: couscous, rice or flat bread, harissa (page 137).

- Heat the oil in a wok or pan and fry the onion for 3–4 minutes over high heat until starting to brown at the edges.
- Add the cinnamon stick, fennel seeds, cayenne or chilli powder, salt and turmeric, and fry for about 10 seconds.

- Add the carrots and potatoes and stir fry for 2 minutes. Stir in the tomato paste and fry for a minute and add the water. Bring to the boil and transfer to the slow cooker.
- Place the cauliflower florets over the top of the vegetables. Cover and switch the slow cooker on to the desired setting.
- About 30 minutes before the end of cooking, gently stir the cauliflower through the curry. Add the curry powder and peas. Stir and cook on High for the remaining time.

Marrakech Vegetable Stew

This colourful, healthy dish doesn't just look beautiful, it tastes wonderful, particularly the next day. The orange juice and apricots add a fruity sweetness and the chopped almonds give the dish a lovely texture against the softness of the vegetables. You can use cashew nuts or macadamias in place of the almonds if you prefer.

Serves 5–6 as a main dish, more as a side dish
Preparation time: 40 minutes
Cook time: 2–3 hours on High | 4–6 hours on Low

5–6 tbsp olive oil
2 medium onions, finely sliced
4–5 cloves of garlic, finely chopped
2 thumb-sized pieces of ginger, grated
2 x 2.5 cm (1 inch) cinnamon sticks
1 tsp fennel seeds
½ tsp turmeric
2 tsp salt or to taste
1 tsp cayenne pepper or to taste
2 medium potatoes, peeled and cut into 2 cm chunks
4 finger aubergines (eggplants), thickly sliced

2 red capsicums, cut into 2.5 cm (1 inch) chunks
2 carrots, halved lengthways and sliced
½ cup chickpeas soaked overnight, drained
6 dried apricots, chopped
2 oranges, juiced
¼ cup blanched chopped almonds
1 tbsp curry powder (page 18) or Ras-el-hanout (page 135)
200 g (7 oz) broccolini or broccoli florets

To serve: couscous, rice or flat bread, harissa (page 137), raita.

- Heat the oil in a wok or large pan and fry the onion for about 2 minutes over high heat. Add the garlic, ginger, cinnamon, and fennel seeds and fry for a further minute.
- Add in the turmeric, salt and cayenne, cook for about 10 seconds and add the potatoes, aubergine (eggplant), capsicums and carrots.

Fry the vegetables for about 2 minutes over high heat. Transfer to the slow cooker.

- Rinse the pan with about half a cup of the water and add to the vegetables together with the chickpeas, apricots and orange juice. Cover and switch the slow cooker on to the desired setting.

- About 20 minutes before the end of cooking, add the almonds, curry powder or Ras-el-hanout and broccolini or broccoli florets. Cook on High for the remaining time.

Slow Cooked Re-fried Bean Burritos

The slow cooker is ideal for cooking beans. Not only is it convenient but the long cooking allows the flavours of all the ingredients to meld together and produce really tasty results. The best Mexican dishes are made with really good, home cooked beans and this easy bean recipe will help you make great enchiladas, burritos, nachos and other vegetarian meals.

The pinto bean is the preferred bean for this dish but black beans, pink beans or kidney beans can be used instead.

Makes 8 Burritos
Preparation time: 10 minutes or less
Cook time: 4–5 hours on High | 8–10 hours on Low

Important Note: Some beans, particularly raw kidney beans, contain a toxin that is only destroyed by boiling. If you are cooking on the Low setting, boil beans for about 10 minutes before draining to ensure that they are safe to eat.

2 cups dried pinto beans
2 tbsp olive oil
2 medium onions, thinly sliced
4–5 cloves of garlic, finely chopped
8 cups (2 litres/3½ pints) hot water

1 bay leaf
1 tsp salt or to taste
½ tsp cayenne or to taste
½ tsp ground cumin (optional)
Juice of 1 lime or lemon

To serve: 8 flour tortillas warmed (page 179), grated cheese, sliced capsicum, sliced avocado, sour cream, sliced spring onions, salsa, taco sauce, sliced jalapenos.

- Pick over the beans, rinse, drain and place in the slow cooker. Heat half the oil in a wok or pan and fry half the onion and half the garlic for about 2 minutes over medium-high heat. Add to the beans in the slow cooker.

- Rinse the pan with a little of the water and add to the cooker with the remaining water and bay leaf. Cover and switch on to the desired setting.
- Drain the beans reserving about half a cup of the cooking liquid, discard the bay leaf and mash the beans using a fork until you have a chunky paste. Mix in the salt, cayenne, cumin if using and half the lime juice.
- When you are ready to assemble the Burritos, heat the remaining oil and fry the remaining onion and garlic gently for 2–3 minutes. Add the beans with a little of the reserved cooking liquid and cook over low heat for about 5 minutes, stirring to avoid the beans sticking to the bottom.
- Taste and adjust the seasoning and lime juice. Serve with warm flour tortillas and preferred toppings; roll up and enjoy.

Bean and Green Chilli Soup with Dumplings

This is a complete, nutritious and tasty meal in a pot and really quick and easy. The dumplings are soft and delicious and ideal for mopping up the sauce.

Serves 5–6
Preparation time: 30 minutes
Cook time: 3–4 hours on High | 6–8 hours on Low

Spice Mix
2 tsp paprika
1 tsp garlic powder
½ tsp freshly ground black pepper
1 tsp dried thyme

2 cups mixed dried beans (pinto,
    kidney, black eyed, haricot,
    chickpea, etc), soaked overnight
2 tbsp sunflower or olive oil
1 large onion, thinly sliced
1 leek, white part only, thinly sliced
    (optional)
3 green banana chillies, diced
3 carrots, diced
4 ripe tomatoes, chopped

8 cups (2 litres/3½ pints) hot
    vegetable or beef stock
2 tsp salt or to taste
1 cup corn kernels, fresh or canned
2 green chillies, finely chopped

Dumplings
¾ cup plain flour
¼ cup coarse cornmeal
½ tsp salt
1 tsp baking powder
1 green chilli, finely chopped
    (optional)
1 medium egg
1 tbsp melted butter or oil
2–3 tbsp cold milk

To serve: nothing but a good appetite and perhaps a little sea salt and freshly cracked pepper.

- Boil the beans for 10 minutes, drain.
- Heat the oil in a wok or pan and sweat the onion, leek if using, banana chillies and carrots over medium heat for 3–4 minutes. Transfer to the slow cooker.
- Add the tomatoes, beans, stock and salt. Cover and switch on to the desired setting.
- Meanwhile combine the dry ingredients for the dumplings in a mixing bowl. Beat the egg and combine with the butter or oil and 2 tbsp milk. Add to the dry ingredients.
- Using a fork, bring the wet and dry ingredients together, adding a little more milk a teaspoon at a time if required, until you have a soft dough. Cover and set aside in a cool place until required.
- About an hour before the end of cooking, stir the spice mix, salt, corn kernels and green chillies into the soup. Turn the slow cooker to the High setting.
- Divide the dumpling dough into 10 equal pieces and, using floured hands, roll into balls, flatten slightly and place on top of the soup. They will sink into the soup but will re-float as they cook.
- Cover and cook without removing the lid for about 45 minutes. Let the soup stand for 10–15 minutes.
- Place 2–3 dumplings in each soup dish and spoon the soup around. Serve immediately.

Creole Bean and Vegetable Soup

For people in and from the Caribbean this thick, tasty soup provides a cheap and nutritious meal. It's very versatile – you can substitute brown rice for the beans, stir in some coconut milk for a richer version and use whatever vegetables are in season.

For a quick version, omit step 2 and just add everything straight into the slow cooker.

Serves 5–6
Preparation time: 30 minutes or less
Cook time: 3–4 hours on High | 6–8 hours on Low

Creole Spice Mix
2 tsp paprika
1 tsp garlic powder
½ tsp freshly ground black pepper
½ tsp onion powder
1 tsp cayenne pepper
½ tsp dried leaf oregano
1 tsp dried thyme

2 cups mixed dried beans (kidney, pinto, chickpeas, black eyed, haricot, etc), soaked overnight
3–4 tbsp sunflower or olive oil

2 medium onions, finely sliced
2 carrots, diced
2 sticks celery, diced
1 small red capsicum, diced
2 medium potatoes, diced
4 ripe tomatoes, chopped
2 cups shredded kale or chard
8 cups (2 litres/3½ pints) hot vegetable or chicken stock
3–4 sprigs fresh thyme (optional)
2 tsp salt or to taste
2 tbsp chopped parsley

To serve: rice or bread, lime wedges.

- Boil the beans for about 10 minutes, drain.
- Heat the oil in a wok or pan and sauté the onions, carrots, celery and capsicum over medium heat for 6–7 minutes. Transfer to the slow cooker with the potatoes, tomatoes, kale, beans and stock. Stir, cover and switch the slow cooker on to the desired setting.
- About 10 minutes before the end of cooking, stir in the fresh thyme if using, spice mix and salt.
- Stir through the chopped parsley just before serving.

10
Quick and Easy Accompaniments

Pilau Rice

Deliciously aromatic and colourful, this rice dish is impressive but easy. Use cochineal and turmeric dissolved in a little hot water if you want to avoid artificial colours.

Serves 4–5

Preparation and cooking time: about 30 minutes.

2 cups basmati rice
1½ tbsp ghee or olive oil
1 tbsp finely chopped onion
8 green cardamom pods
2 x 2.5 cm (1 inch) cinnamon sticks
4 cloves

2 bay leaves
3 cups (750 ml/1¼ pints) cold water
1 level tsp salt
¼ tsp red food colouring
¼ tsp yellow food colouring

- Wash the rice in several changes of water and leave to drain in a large sieve.
- Pre-heat the oven to 170°C, 325°F or gas mark 3.
- Meanwhile, heat the ghee or oil in a heavy based pan with a tight fitting lid, and fry the onion until just translucent.
- Add the cardamoms, cinnamon, cloves, and bay leaves and cook for 1 minute.
- Add the drained rice and mix well to coat all the grains with the ghee or oil. Cook on medium heat for about a minute.
- Stir in the water and salt and bring to the boil. Once boiling, turn the heat to very low and place the lid on the pan.

- Stir the rice after about 5 minutes, and again after 3 minutes. Re-cover and leave for a further 4–5 minutes after which time all the water will have been absorbed.
- If using powdered food colourings, mix each one with about a tablespoonful of water, keeping the two colours separate.
- Spoon two or three "blobs" of each colour onto the rice. Replace the lid and place the pan in the oven for about 20 minutes to dry off the rice and set the colours.
- Fluff up with a fork and serve.

Steamed Jasmine Rice

This is really easy and perfect with Thai curries.

Serves 4–5
Preparation and cooking time: 20 minutes

2½ cups Thai Jasmine rice
3 cups (750 ml/1¼ pints) water
Large pinch of salt (optional)

- Place the rice in a smallish, heavy based saucepan with a tight fitting lid (capacity of about 2 litres/4½ pints). Cover with plenty of cold water, stir well and drain. Repeat twice more.
- Add the 3 cups of water, the salt if used, and bring to the boil over medium heat. Stir, turn the heat down to as low as you can and cover the pan. Cook for about 10 minutes until all the water has been absorbed.
- Turn off the heat and let the rice stand for a further 5 minutes. Fluff up lightly with a fork and serve hot.

Jamaican Rice and Peas

Serves 5–6
Preparation time: 10 minutes or less
Cook time: Less than 20 minutes

2 cups long grain rice
400 ml (14 fl oz) coconut milk
1 small onion, finely chopped
1 clove of garlic, finely chopped
2 sprigs of fresh thyme or ¼ tsp dried

½ tsp salt
1 habanero chilli, whole
1 cup frozen peas (or canned kidney
  beans)

- Wash the rice in three or four changes of water and drain. Place in a medium saucepan with a tight fitting lid.
- Add enough water to the coconut milk to make 4 cups (1 litre/1¾ pints) and add to the rice together with all the other ingredients.
- Bring to the boil, stirring, cover the pan and turn the heat down to as low as possible. Cook for about 12 minutes, stirring twice.
- Let the rice stand for a further 5 minutes, remove the whole chilli and serve.

Saffron, Raisin and Fresh Mint Couscous

Serves 4–5

Preparation and cooking time: 10 minutes or less (plus standing time)

1½ cups (375 ml/12 fl oz) hot water
Large pinch saffron threads
1 tbsp raisins
2 tsp extra virgin olive oil

¼ tsp salt or to taste
1½ cups couscous
2–3 tbsp chopped fresh mint

- Place the water, saffron and raisins in a medium saucepan, cover and set aside for about 30 minutes.
- Bring the mixture to the boil, and stir in the olive oil, salt and couscous. Remove from the heat, cover again and let stand for 10–12 minutes.
- Fluff the couscous and break the lumps to separate the grains using a fork. Stir in the mint and serve.

Apricot, Almond and Orange Couscous

- Omit the saffron and raisins in the above recipe and replace with 2 tbsp chopped dried apricots and proceed as above. Stir in 1 tbsp slivered almonds and 1 tbsp finely shredded orange zest. Do not add mint.

Nan

Making good nan bread is really easy, particularly if you have a bread maker. Just put everything into the bread pan and let the bread maker knead for about 5 minutes only – just enough to provide a smooth dough. You can leave the dough to rise in the bread pan with the machine switched off.

The dough can be stored in the fridge for up to two days. It will rise, quite quickly at first until it cools down, so check it frequently and punch it down.

Makes 6 nan

Preparation time: 10 minutes plus about an hour to prove the dough

300 ml (10 fl oz) water (approximately)
2 tsp sugar
2 tsp instant dried yeast
1 tbsp oil

450 g (1 lb) white bread flour or
  plain white flour
1 tsp salt
Extra flour for dusting

- Warm the water slightly, pour into a large bowl and add the sugar, yeast and oil.
- Add the flour and sprinkle the salt over the flour. Using your hand, mix and bring the ingredients together, adding more water or more flour until you have a soft but non-sticky dough.
- Place the dough onto a clean, lightly floured surface and knead it for about 5 minutes until smooth.
- Place the dough in a lightly greased bowl, cover with a damp tea towel or greased cling wrap. Place the bowl in a draught free place for about an hour or until the dough has doubled in size.
- De-gas the dough by punching it down and knead briefly. Divide into 6 equal portions and roll into balls.
- Using a little flour for dusting, roll into a thin round or tear shape and cook on a hot tawa or frying pan for about 2 minutes each side. Brown spots should appear and the nan should puff up.
- Alternatively, cook underside on the tawa and place under a very hot grill for about a minute to cook to the top.
- Wrap in a clean tea towel to keep warm while cooking the remaining nan.
- Brush with oil and serve.

Puri

These deep fried little flat breads can be made with white or wholewheat flour and are a good choice if you are cooking for a large number of people as they are quick and easy to make and re-heat well.

Makes 18–20
Preparation and cooking time: 30 minutes

450 g (1 lb) chapati, wholewheat or plain flour plus extra for dusting
1 tsp salt

Oil for deep frying

- Place the flour in a large mixing bowl, sprinkle with the salt and slowly add about 220 ml (8 fl oz) of water, mixing the flour and water together until you have a soft, pliable dough.
- Using damp hands, knead the dough briefly, fold into a neat shape, cover and set aside for 10–15 minutes.
- Fill a karahi, wok or deep saucepan about two thirds full of oil and heat the oil to hot but not smoking.
- Take a piece of dough about the size of a golf ball and roll into a round about 15 cm (6 inches) in diameter and about 1 mm thick. Repeat with 3–5 more pieces of dough depending on the size of your karahi.
- Quickly slide the puris into the hot oil. They should rise to the surface within about 6 seconds and begin to puff up. As they do, gently flip them over for a few seconds to lightly brown the other side. The whole process should take about 15 seconds.
- Remove the puris and drain them on a wire rack placed over a tray. Repeat with the remaining dough.
- Serve immediately or wrap in foil.
- Reheat for a few seconds in the microwave or place on a baking tray, cover with foil and place in a hot oven.

Bhatura

- Proceed as for puri but use plain yogurt to make the dough in place of water.

Flour Tortilla

There is nothing like Fajitas with fresh, warm home-made tortillas. With my tips for rolling them out thinly, they're quite easy to make and can be made ahead.

Makes 8

Preparation and cooking time 20 minutes (plus resting time for dough)

2½ cups plain flour

1 tsp bicarbonate of soda

1 tsp salt

1 tsp oil

1 cup (250 ml/8 fl oz) milk
(approximately)

Extra flour for dusting

2 tbsp (approximately) extra oil

- Place all the dry ingredients into a mixing bowl and drizzle over the oil. Gradually add the milk, bringing the liquid and flour together with your fingertips to form a soft but non-sticky dough. Knead lightly until smooth, cover and allow to rest for about 10 minutes.
- Using floured hands, divide the dough into eight portions and roll each portion into a ball. Place on a lightly floured board or plate and keep covered with a damp tea towel.
- Place a tawa, heavy based frying pan or skillet on the stove on medium-high heat.
- Take two balls and roll each one out to about the size of a small saucer. Spread about a teaspoon or two of oil onto one round taking the oil right out to the edge and sprinkle over about two teaspoons of flour, making sure the oil is lightly but completely covered. A flour dredger is good for doing this.
- Place the second round on top and press down lightly. Dust with flour again and roll into a thin round about 22 cm (9 inches) in diameter.
- Cook for about 15–20 seconds each side. The tortillas should bubble up a little and pale brown spots will appear on the underside. The two rounds will also separate from each other around the edges.
- Pull the two rounds apart – they will pull apart quite easily – and cook the uncooked side of each tortilla for a further 15 seconds or so. You will now have two thin flour tortillas. Wrap in a napkin or clean tea towel and repeat with the remaining dough.
- When ready to eat, you can warm the tortillas in the microwave for a few seconds or in the oven wrapped in foil.

Fijian Raita

Serves 4–5
Preparation time: 5 minutes

2 cups (500 ml/18 fl oz pint) thick
   Greek style yogurt
1 carrot, grated
½ cucumber, grated
1 tbsp finely chopped onion

1 clove of garlic, finely chopped
1 green chilli, finely chopped
1 tsp cumin seeds
½ tsp salt or to taste
Freshly ground pepper to taste

- Combine all the ingredients and mix well. Cover and refrigerate for an hour or so to let the flavours develop.

Indian Raita

2 cups (500 ml/18 fl oz) plain yogurt
½ red onion, finely sliced
½ cucumber, grated
½ white radish, grated
1 small clove of garlic, finely chopped
1 green chilli, finely chopped

½ tsp salt (or to taste)
½ tsp cumin seeds
½ tsp garam masala
1 tbsp chopped fresh coriander
Pinch turmeric (optional)

- Combine all the ingredients in a large bowl and stir until well mixed. Refrigerate until required.

Coconut Chutney

2 cups grated fresh coconut
Small bunch of coriander, coarsely chopped
1 green chilli, coarsely chopped

2 tsp grated ginger
3 tablespoons lemon juice
1 tsp salt

- Combine all the ingredients in the bowl of a food processor and process until finely chopped. Allow the flavours to develop for an hour or so before serving.

Kasundi
(Indian Hot Tomato Relish)

I have yet to meet anyone who doesn't become addicted to this delicious tomato based relish. It is rich, intensely aromatic and quite unlike any other you may have eaten before. A mix of fragrant, heady Indian spices cooked in hot oil blend harmoniously to create a mysterious depth of amazing flavours. The kasundi is eaten with Indian meals like any other Indian pickle or chutney, but it will also provide a lip smacking lift to chicken, burgers, sausages and even sandwiches.

There are many variations of the basic recipe. This one is quite authentic in appearance and flavour and really easy to make in your slow cooker.

Makes about 1.5 litres/3¼ pints
Preparation time: 30 minutes
Cook time: 2–3 hours on High / 4–6 hours on Low

Spice Mix
1½ tbsp yellow mustard seeds
1 tbsp fenugreek seeds
1 tbsp black cumin seeds
2 tsp fennel seeds
2 tsp ground cumin
2 tbsp turmeric
1 tbsp chilli powder

10 large cloves of garlic, roughly chopped

3 thumb-sized pieces of ginger, roughly chopped
6 hot green or red chillies, roughly chopped
1.5 kg (3 lb) Roma style tomatoes, chopped
400 ml (14 fl oz) malt vinegar
200 ml (7 fl oz) olive or sunflower oil
½ cup grated palm or soft brown sugar
1 tbsp salt

- Process the garlic, ginger and chillies until finely chopped. Place half the chopped tomatoes in a food processor or blender, add about half the vinegar and process until fairly smooth. Repeat with the remaining tomato and vinegar.
- Heat the oil in a wok or large pan until very hot but not smoking. Turn the heat down a little and add the spice mix. Cook, stirring, for

about 2 minutes until the mixture darkens a little and becomes deeply aromatic. Take care not to burn it or it will become bitter.

- Add the garlic and ginger mixture and stir fry over medium to high heat for 1½ minutes or until aromatic.
- Add the processed tomato, sugar and salt and stir until sugar dissolves. Bring to the boil and simmer for 2 or 3 minutes. Foam will form at the surface. Skim this off and discard. Don't worry if you don't get it all.
- Transfer the mixture carefully to the slow cooker, cover and switch on. Stir half way through cooking.
- Kasundi is ready when it develops a jam like appearance and the oil rises to the top.
- The kasundi will keep in the fridge for up to 4 weeks or indefinitely if transferred whilst still hot into sterilised jars and sealed.

Recipe Notes:
- There appears to be a lot of oil on the surface whilst the kasundi is still in the slow cooker. Don't worry about this as once it is transferred into jars there is just enough oil on top to keep the kasundi fresh for several weeks.
- A kasundi cooked in the slow cooker will not be quite as thick as one cooked on top of the stove. I don't feel that this a problem but if you want it thicker, cook with the lid off, stirring once or twice, for the last hour. Remember, it will thicken further on cooling.
- It is important to use Roma or egg tomatoes as these don't have as much liquid as salad tomatoes.

Index

Three ways to order *Right Way* books:

1.   Visit www.constablerobinson.com and order through our website.

2.   Telephone the TBS order line on 01206 255 800.
     Order lines are open Monday – Friday, 8:30am – 5:30pm.

3.   Use this order form and send a cheque made payable to TBS Ltd or charge my
     [ ] Visa   [ ] Mastercard   [ ] Maestro (issue no   )

Card number: _____

Expiry date: _____ Last three digits on back of card: _____

Signature: _____
(your signature is essential when paying by credit or debit card)

No. of copies	Title	Price	Total
	The Curry Secret	£5.99	
	The New Curry Secret	£7.99	
	Thai Cookery Secrets	£5.99	
	For P&P add £2.75 for the first book, 60p for each additional book		
	Grand Total		£

Name: _____

Address: _____

_____ Postcode: _____

Daytime Tel. No./Email _____
(in case of query)

Please return forms to Cash Sales/Direct Mail Dept., The Book Service, Colchester Road, Frating Green, Colchester CO7 7DW.

Enquiries to readers@constablerobinson.com.

Constable and Robinson Ltd (directly or via its agents) may mail, email or phone you about promotions or products.

[ ] Tick box if you do not want these from us [ ] or our subsidiaries.

www.constablerobinson.com/rightway